Impact Listening 2

Jill Robbins
Andrew MacNeill

Series Editor **Michael Rost**

Longman

Published by
Longman Asia ELT
2/F Cornwall House
Taikoo Place
979 King's Road
Quarry Bay
Hong Kong

fax: +852 2856 9578
e-mail: aelt@pearsoned.com.hk
www.longman.com

and Associated Companies throughout the world.

This book was developed for Longman Asia ELT by Lateral Communications Limited.

First published 2001
Reprinted by Pearson Education Asia Limited 2005 (twice)

Produced by Pearson Education Asia Limited, Hong Kong
GCC/17

PROJECT DIRECTOR, SERIES EDITOR: Michael Rost
PROJECT COORDINATOR: Keiko Kimura
PROJECT EDITORS: Terry Passero, Jenny Lorant, Anne McGannon Louis, Wendy Mazzoni
ART DIRECTOR: Lisa Ekström
DESIGN: Lisa Ekström, Keiko Kimura

PRODUCTION COORDINATOR: Eric Yau
ILLUSTRATIONS: Frank Ansley, Anna Vetlfort, Gary Hallgren, Glenn Dudley, Jody Jobe
PHOTOGRAPHS: Mark Johann, Fox Images, PhotoDisc
RECORDING COORDINATOR: Ellen Schwartz
RECORDING ENGINEERS: Mary Ellen Perry, Glenn Davidson, David Joslyn
MUSIC: Music Bakery
WEBSITE COORDINATOR: John Cunha

The publisher's policy is to use **paper manufactured from sustainable forests**

IMPACT LISTENING 1
Student Book + Self Study CD ISBN 962 00 51335
Teacher's Manual   ISBN 962 00 5136X
Classroom Cassettes Set   ISBN 962 00 51394
Classroom CD Set   ISBN 962 00 51424
Impact Listening 1 Test Pack ISBN 962 00 51459

IMPACT LISTENING 2
Student Book + Self Study CD ISBN 962 00 51343
Teacher's Manual   ISBN 962 00 51378
Classroom Cassettes Set   ISBN 962 00 51408
Classroom CD set   ISBN 962 00 51432
Impact Listening 2 Test Pack ISBN 962 00 51467

IMPACT LISTENING 3
Student Book + Self Study CD ISBN 962 00 51351
Teacher's Manual   ISBN 962 00 51386
Classroom Cassettes Set   ISBN 962 00 51416
Classroom CD set   ISBN 962 00 51440
Impact Listening 3 Test Pack ISBN 962 00 51475

Acknowledgements

The authors, editors, and publishers would like to thank the following people who contributed so much to the development of the *Impact Listening* series: First, we would like to thank the many language teachers around the world who reviewed and piloted earlier versions of the textbooks:

Anthony Butera	Kyoko Kawagoe	Maggie Sokolik
Jennifer Bixby	An-Ran Kim	Dianne Stark
Karen Carrier	Ellen Kisslinger	Jim Swan
Andrea Carvalho	Masayoshi	Judy Tanka
Neil Cowie	Kobayashi	Donna Tatsuki
Terry Cox	Mike Laib	John Thompson
Christopher Decker	Elizabeth Lange	Joe Tomei
John Doodigain	Ruth Larimer	George Truscott
Bill Figoni	Nyla Marnay	Carol Vaughn
Tamotsu Fujita	Michael Mew	Larry Vandergrift
Masayoshi Fukui	Akiko Mizoguchi	Susan Vik
Michael Glaser	Yuko Nakajima	Daniel Walsh
Ann Gleason	William Newman	Kirk Wiltshire
Erik Gunderson	Yuko Ono	Jerry Winn
Naoya Hase	Allison Peck	Julie Winter
Louise Haynes	Arturo Pedroso	Dennis Woolbright
Jane Hoelker	Joyce Rossignol	Carolyn Wu
Philip Houerkamp	Elly Schottman	Yoko Yamazaki

We would like to give special thanks to our colleagues at Pearson Education who provided support and useful feedback during the development of the series:

Joanne Dresner	Craig Zettle	Kate Lowe
Dugie Cameron	Nick Lutz	Karen Fraser
Karen Chiang	Allen Ascher	Chongdae Chung
Eleanor Barnes	Louisa Hellegers	Marion Cooper
Mieko Otaka	Tom Sweeney	

Many people contributed to the shaping of the extracts for *Impact Listening* and participated in the authentic recordings on which the final recordings were based, or took part in the actual studio drafts and final recordings:

Hamed Abdel-Samad	Katie Hemmeter	Cheryl Roorda
Laura Jean Anderson	Alex Kahn	Jason Ramey
Melody Albie	Paul Kent	Ellen Schwartz
Selana Allen	Rick Kappra	Eric Damon Smith
Cassidy Brown	Charisse Loriaux	Irma Spars
Catherine Burriss	Jason Lewis	James Seger
Mark Brosamer	Tom Lam	Jerome Schwab
Melody Bryant	Christina Morrell	Kamala Stroup
Feodor Chin	Patricia Mulholland	Micah Schraft
Peter Canavese	Purni Morell	Micah Scott
Chris Cooper	Rami Margron	Diane Tasca
Sarah Cox	Tony Montemayor	Paul Thompson
Jennifer Dennison	Carrie Olson	Rick Tabor
Lisa Fredericksen	Colleen Oakes	Stephanie Taylor
Nathan Falstreau	Daniel Olmstead	Germaine Ventura
David Gassner	Joy Osmanski	Edward Wallace
Justin Good	Amy Parker	Julie Wulferdingen
Scott Grinthal	Bill Parry	Paul Wiesser
Albert Hodge	Heather Pierce	Cesar Zepeda
Erin Henning	Jackie Pels	
	Michelle Powell	
	Rachel Peters	

Special thanks to Jason Lewis, Expedition 360, Hardscratch Press, 3: woman chord, and the rock group, Pink!

Introduction

The *Impact Listening* series is an innovative series of teaching materials to help learners develop listening and speaking ability. The series has three levels:

Impact Listening 1 (for beginners)
Impact Listening 2 (for high beginners)
Impact Listening 3 (for intermediate and advanced students)

There are five main principles on which the *Impact Listening* series is based:

1. Rich input

Learners need **rich input** in order to develop their language ability. The best input is **contextualized**, **based on authentic sources** and **interesting** for the learners. Input that is **slightly above the learners' proficiency level** provides a challenge to motivate learners. *Impact Listening* features extracts drawn from or based on authentic conversations and uses a wide variety of speakers to provide an abundance of interesting input.

2. Clear tasks

In order to develop their attention span, learners need guidance in **what to listen for**. Clear **tasks** guide the student in what to focus on and what to remember. **Task cycles** allow students to **listen to the same input more than once**, in order to practice controlling their attention. Each section in *Impact Listening* provides a transparent, structured task that is easy to use in the classroom.

3. Listening strategies

In order to become more confident and relaxed, learners need to learn **how to listen**. By using successful listening strategies — **predicting**, **inferring**, **clarifying**, and **responding**, learners will become more "fluent listeners." By **explicitly** including strategy instruction in the classroom, teachers encourage their students to learn more efficiently. These strategies are taught consistently throughout the *Impact Listening* series.

4. Language awareness

Listening provides an important opportunity for learners to experience language "in **real time**." By helping students **focus on form while listening**, teachers can help students acquire a deeper understanding of grammar and vocabulary. Each unit in Impact Listening provides a Language Awareness activity to maximize learning from listening.

5. Self-expression

The central purpose of listening is application — using the ideas in the conversation and formulating some kind of response. By incorporating **self-expression** steps with listening activities, students increase their overall oral language ability. *Impact Listening* features a variety of short speaking activities as well as an extended Interaction Link in each unit to build conversational skills alongside listening skills.

The unit design of *Impact Listening* allows for clear implementation of these principles. Each unit has four main sections: **Vocabulary Task, Listening Task, Real World Listening**, and **Language Awareness** plus an **Interaction Link** and a **Self-Study Page** in the Appendix. All activities are designed to be easy to use in any classroom setting.

Unit Components

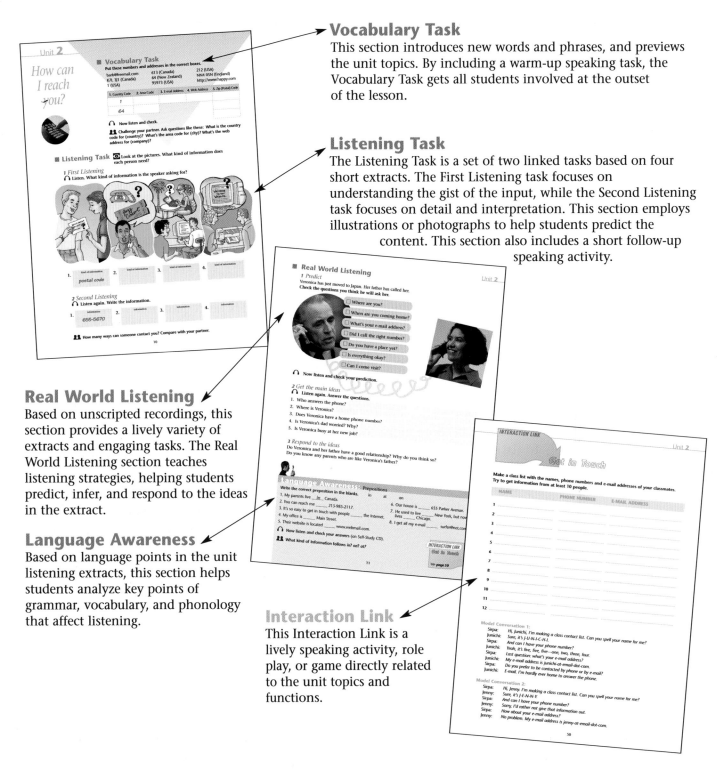

Vocabulary Task

This section introduces new words and phrases, and previews the unit topics. By including a warm-up speaking task, the Vocabulary Task gets all students involved at the outset of the lesson.

Listening Task

The Listening Task is a set of two linked tasks based on four short extracts. The First Listening task focuses on understanding the gist of the input, while the Second Listening task focuses on detail and interpretation. This section employs illustrations or photographs to help students predict the content. This section also includes a short follow-up speaking activity.

Real World Listening

Based on unscripted recordings, this section provides a lively variety of extracts and engaging tasks. The Real World Listening section teaches listening strategies, helping students predict, infer, and respond to the ideas in the extract.

Language Awareness

Based on language points in the unit listening extracts, this section helps students analyze key points of grammar, vocabulary, and phonology that affect listening.

Interaction Link

This Interaction Link is a lively speaking activity, role play, or game directly related to the unit topics and functions.

Self-Study Page

For use with the Self-Study CD, the Self-Study Page provides new tasks for the Real World Listening extract, to allow students to review at home. The Self Study CD also contains the Language Awareness section, for at-home review.

Teacher's Manual

Teachers are encouraged to utilize the *Impact Listening* Teacher's Manual. This manual contains teaching procedures, insightful language and culture notes, full scripts, answer keys, expansion activities, and review tests.

Web Site

Teachers and students are welcome to use the Impact series website for additional ideas and resources.

<www.impactseries.com/listening>

To the Student

Impact Listening will help you use listening strategies. Listening strategies are ways of thinking actively as you listen. Here are the main strategies you will practice in this course:

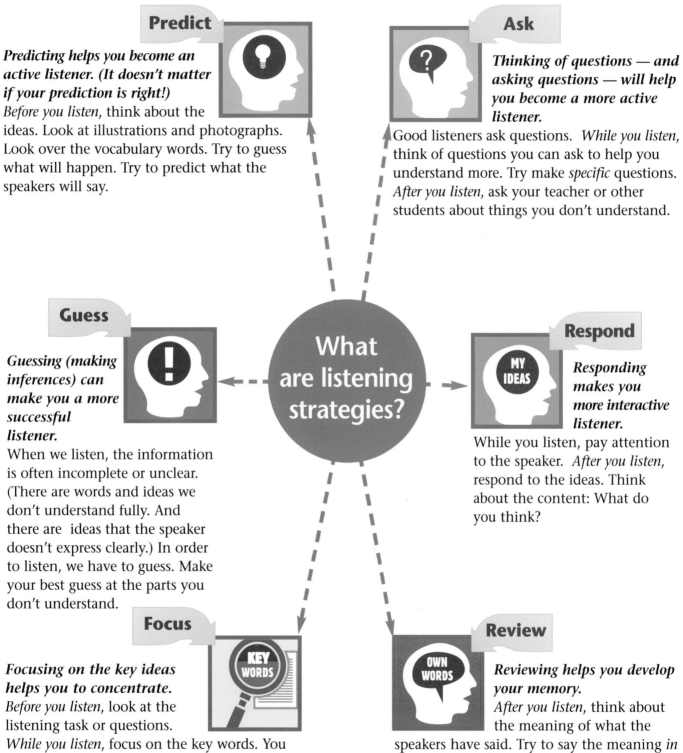

Predict

Predicting helps you become an active listener. (It doesn't matter if your prediction is right!)
Before you listen, think about the ideas. Look at illustrations and photographs. Look over the vocabulary words. Try to guess what will happen. Try to predict what the speakers will say.

Ask

Thinking of questions — and asking questions — will help you become a more active listener.
Good listeners ask questions. *While you listen*, think of questions you can ask to help you understand more. Try make *specific* questions. *After you listen*, ask your teacher or other students about things you don't understand.

Guess

Guessing (making inferences) can make you a more successful listener.
When we listen, the information is often incomplete or unclear. (There are words and ideas we don't understand fully. And there are ideas that the speaker doesn't express clearly.) In order to listen, we have to guess. Make your best guess at the parts you don't understand.

Respond

Responding makes you more interactive listener.
While you listen, pay attention to the speaker. *After you listen*, respond to the ideas. Think about the content: What do you think?

Focus

Focusing on the key ideas helps you to concentrate.
Before you listen, look at the listening task or questions.
While you listen, focus on the key words. You don't have to understand every word. Use the words you understand. Try to form a main idea. If there are some words you don't understand, that's OK. Keep listening.

Review

Reviewing helps you develop your memory.
After you listen, think about the meaning of what the speakers have said. Try to say the meaning *in your own words*.

Contents

Unit Number	Theme	Title	Vocabulary Task	Listening Task	Real World Listening	Language Awareness	Interaction Link
11	Travel pages 28 - 29	*They lost my luggage!*	Problems when traveling	Identifying problems that arise while traveling	A man describes an unusual trip to Costa Rica	Reduced forms and assimilations	The Terrible Trip Game: *board game*
12	Business pages 30 - 31	*Check this out!*	Machines needed for work	Understanding the functions of new technologies	Two men talk about pros and cons of working from home	Two-part verbs	Internet Business: *Setting up an Internet business*
13	Schedules pages 32 - 33	*I can squeeze you in...*	Schedules and commitments	Arranging a schedule	A band's manager explains the band's upcoming schedule	Prepositions for time	Making Plans: *Arranging a time to meet with a friend*
14	Weather pages 34 - 35	*It was a real scorcher!*	Descriptions of weather	Understanding weather forecasts	A grandmother and grandson talk about the weather in Alaska	Idioms related to weather	The Four Seasons Game: *A vocabulary game*
15	Entertainment pages 36 - 37	*I couldn't say no!*	Expressions for offering and responding to invitations	Understanding invitations and reasons declining invitations	An employee talks about unusual invitations at work	Politeness in invitations	Let's Party: *Inviting classmates to a party*
16	Home pages 38 - 39	*It's just like living on Earth*	Areas to live and qualities of those areas	Defining qualities of areas to live	A reporter interviews a woman who lives on a space station	Count and non-count nouns	Space Station: *Designing the living areas on a space station*
17	Health pages 40 - 41	*I'll try anything!*	Alternative remedies for illnesses	Understanding symptoms and treatments for physical problems	A relaxation exercise involving music and visualization	Verb phrases associated with health	Home Remedies: *Sharing personal remedies for common health problems*
18	Shopping pages 42 - 43	*Shopping here is so exciting!*	Shopping and services	Distinguishing cultural differences about shopping	Two women are shopping in an African market	Idioms related to money	Let's Make a Deal: *Bargaining for the best price*
19	Food pages 44 - 45	*What'd you get?*	Tastes and qualities of food	Identifying ingredients in dishes	Two people describe the "strange" foods they are eating	Idioms related to food	Try It—You'll Like It: *Describing exotic foods*
20	News pages 46 - 47	*This just in...*	Common news stories	Understanding different opinions on an issue	Students discuss an issue in the news	Language of news headlines	News Debate: *Discussing a current topic*

You'll really like him

■ Vocabulary Task

🎧 **Listen to the introductions. Match them with the responses.**

INTRODUCTION

_c_ 1. Hello, my name is ...
___ 2. This is my friend ...
___ 3. I'd like to introduce...
___ 4. Have you met ...?
___ 5. I'd like you to meet ...
___ 6. Dad, this is ...

RESPONSE

a. It's a pleasure to meet you, Ms. Williams.
b. Hey, Taka. How's it going?
c. Hi, Elizabeth. I'm Jason.
d. It's nice to meet you.
e. Oh, yeah, we have met. How are you?
f. Good to meet you.

👥 **Now introduce your partner to another pair of students. Then your partner should introduce you. Keep going!**

■ Listening Task 👁 Look at the pictures. Where are the people?

1 First Listening

🎧 **Listen. What introductions do they use?**

1. This is... 2. 3. 4.

2 Second Listening

🎧 **Listen again. Check the responses.**

1.	2.	3.	4.
✔ It's a pleasure to meet you.	☐ Pleased to meet you.	☐ It's my pleasure.	☐ Good to meet you.
☐ Hi, how are you doing?	☐ Hey, Norma!	☐ Oh, yeah, we've met.	☐ Hi, Kathy.

👥 **Look at each expression above. Which ones are formal? Which ones are informal? How are they different?**

■ **Real World Listening**

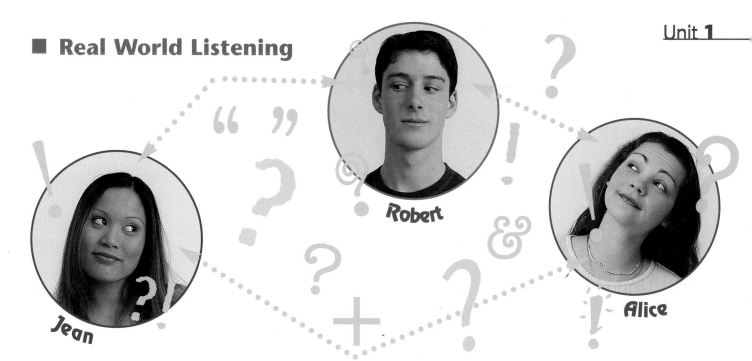

Robert

Alice

Jean

1 Predict

What are the relationships between Jean, Alice and Robert? Check your guesses.

- ☐ Jean is interested in Robert.
- ☐ Robert is interested in Alice.
- ☐ Alice wants to go out with Robert.
- ☐ Alice is Jean's friend.
- ☐ Jean is Robert's sister.
- ☐ other? _____

🎧 **Now listen to the conversation.**

2 Get the main ideas

🎧 **Listen again. Write *T* (True), *F* (False), or *?* (I don't know) for each statement.**

- T Alice likes Robert.
- F Robert is interested in Alice.
- T Alice introduces Jean to Robert.
- T Jean thinks Robert is handsome.
- F Jean is going out with Sam.
- T Robert is interested in Jean.
- T Jean and Robert have met before.

3 Respond to the ideas

What do you think will happen next?
What do you think of this situation?

Language Awareness: Short Words

Read these introductions. Fill in the missing words.

1. I'd like _to_ introduce _you_ _to_ my friend Alan.

2. Pleased _to_ meet you, Alan.

3. It _is_ nice _to_ meet you, too, Mr. Gray.

4. _Do_ _you_ met Ellen?

5. No, not yet. It _is_ _a_ pleasure _to_ meet you, Ellen.

6. My name _is_ Bob Wells.

🎧 **Now listen and check your answers.**

👥 How are these words pronounced in conversations: *to, is, have, you, a?*

INTERACTION LINK

Meet the Class

➡ *page 49*

How can I reach you?

■ Vocabulary Task

Put these numbers and addresses in the correct boxes.

barb@freemail.com   613 (Canada)   212 (USA)
K7L 3J1 (Canada)   64 (New Zealand)   NN4 0SN (England)
1 (USA)   95973 (USA)   http://www.happy.com

1. Country Code	2. Area Code	3. E-mail Address	4. Web Address	5. Zip (Postal) Code
1				
64				

∩ Now listen and check.

 Challenge your partner. Ask questions like these: What is the country code for (country)? What's the area code for (city)? What's the web address for (company)?

■ Listening Task ◉ Look at the pictures. What kind of information does each person need?

1 First Listening
∩ Listen. What kind of information is the speaker asking for?

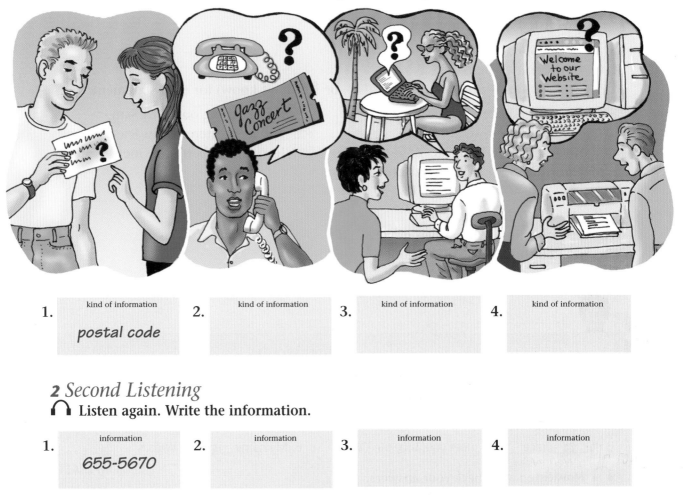

1. kind of information

postal code

2. kind of information

3. kind of information

4. kind of information

2 Second Listening
∩ Listen again. Write the information.

1. information

655-5670

2. information

3. information

4. information

How many ways can someone contact you? Compare with your partner.

■ Real World Listening

1 Predict

Veronica has just moved to Japan. Her father has called her.
Check the questions you think he will ask her.

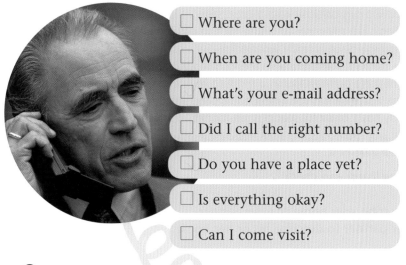

☐ Where are you?

☐ When are you coming home?

☐ What's your e-mail address?

☐ Did I call the right number?

☐ Do you have a place yet?

☐ Is everything okay?

☐ Can I come visit?

🎧 Now listen and check your prediction.

2 Get the main ideas

🎧 Listen again. Answer the questions.

1. Who answers the phone?

2. Where is Veronica?

3. Does Veronica have a home phone number?

4. Is Veronica's dad worried? Why?

5. Is Veronica busy at her new job?

3 Respond to the ideas

Do Veronica and her father have a good relationship? Why do you think so?
Do you know any parents who are like Veronica's father?

Language Awareness: Prepositions

Write the correct preposition in the blanks.   in   at   on

1. My parents live __in__ Canada.

2. You can reach me _____ 213-985-2117.

3. It's so easy to get in touch with people _____ the Internet.

4. My office is _____ Main Street.

5. Their website is located _____ www.webmail.com.

6. Our house is _____ 655 Parker Avenue.

7. He used to live _____ New York, but now he lives _____ Chicago.

8. I get all my e-mail _____ surfer@net.com.

🎧 Now listen and check your answers.

👥 What kind of information follows *in? on? at?*

INTERACTION LINK
Get in Touch

➡ *page 50*

Don't you wish we could live here?

■ Vocabulary Task

**Read these statements. Write + for something they like (positive).
Write – for something they don't like (negative).**

1. — I don't like the place I live now. It's too isolated.
2. ___ I have a big balcony with a great view. I love it!
3. ___ I don't like my parents' house. It's so old-fashioned.
4. ___ Her new place is really wonderful — it's so roomy.
5. ___ He thinks it's important to feel comfortable in a home.
6. ___ I think it's great to live in a modern building, don't you?
7. ___ This apartment is too cramped. It's too small for our family.
8. ___ Amy has a beautiful spacious loft for her art studio. She's really happy there.
9. ___ Bill and Sherry have a nice, cozy little apartment in the city. They call it their love nest.

🎧 Now listen and check.

👥 Describe your home to your partner.
Ask your partner to describe his or her home.

■ Listening Task 👁 Look at the pictures. Describe each place.

1 First Listening

🎧 Listen. What kind of place would each speaker like to have?

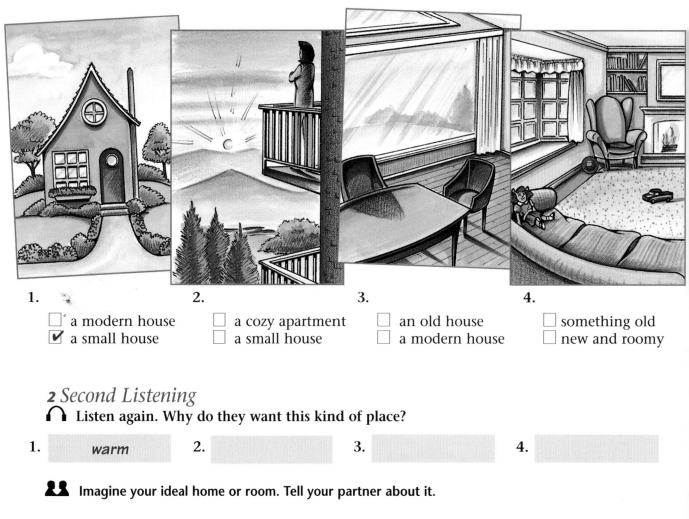

1.

☐ a modern house
☑ a small house

2.

☐ a cozy apartment
☐ a small house

3.

☐ an old house
☐ a modern house

4.

☐ something old
☐ new and roomy

2 Second Listening

🎧 Listen again. Why do they want this kind of place?

1. *warm*   2.   3.   4.

👥 Imagine your ideal home or room. Tell your partner about it.

■ Real World Listening

1 Predict

John and Diane live in a small apartment. Tonight they're at a party at a large house.

What do you think they will like about the place?

___ it's spacious   ___ it has a view   ___ it's comfortable

___ it has modern furniture   ___ it has a balcony   ___ other? _____

🎧 **Now listen to the conversation.**

2 Get the main ideas

🎧 **Listen again. Answer the questions.**

1. What is the house like inside?

2. What is the house like outside?

3. What does Diane like about the house?

4. What does John dislike about the house?

3 Respond to the ideas

What do Diane and John disagree about?
What is more important to you: the way your place looks or the way it feels?

Language Awareness: Modifiers

Underline the modifier in each sentence.

1. Our place is <u>too</u> isolated.

2. This place is unbelievably cool.

3. Her house is kind of old fashioned.

4. Their new house is way too expensive.

5. We were sort of cramped in our last place.

6. That's an extremely large balcony.

🎧 **Now listen and check your answers.**

👥 **Which modifiers make the meaning stronger? Weaker?**

INTERACTION LINK
My Place

➡ *page 51*

13

It means a lot to me

■ Vocabulary Task

What accessories can you see in this picture?

Bracelet   Necklace   Ring   Earrings   Watch   Pin   Scarf

🎧   **Why do people wear certain accessories? Listen and match.**

_b_ 1. Henna tattoos   a. *To protect me*
___ 2. Leather ring   b. *For fun*
___ 3. Rakari bracelet   c. *Friends said it has special powers*
___ 4. Silk scarf   d. *Grandmother gave it to me*
___ 5. Digital watch   e. *Has a lot of sentimental value*
___ 6. Crystal necklace   f. *Makes me look good*
___ 7. Silver pin   g. *Reminds me of appointments*

👥 **Look around the room. How many accessories can you see?**

■ Listening Task 👁 Look at the pictures. What accessories are they wearing?

1 First Listening

🎧   Listen. Some people are talking about accessories they own.
Write the name of the accessory and what it's made of.

1.	2.	3.	4.
rakari cloth			

2 Second Listening

🎧   Listen again. Why does the person wear the accessory?

1.	2.	3.	4.
☑ a. to protect him	☐ a. she believes in crystals	☐ a. it has sentimental value	☐ a. it's something special
☐ b. his sister gave it to him	☐ b. she likes the way it looks	☐ b. it's an interesting ring	☐ b. it makes him look good

👥 **Talk about an accessory you have. Does it have sentimental value? Is it a gift from someone?**

■ Real World Listening

1 Predict

Chandra is telling a friend about a special necklace.
Guess her reason for wearing it.

☐ Her mother gave it to her, so it has sentimental value.

☐ It protects her from illness.

☐ It's very expensive.

🎧 **Now listen to the conversation.**

2 Get the main ideas

🎧 **Listen again.**
Complete the sentences.

The necklace is made of

_____.

_____ told her to

wear it. _____ gave it to her.

When she took the necklace off, _____. When she put it back on,

_____.

3 Respond to the ideas

Chandra says the necklace has a special power. Do you believe that objects can have special powers? Do you know of any other objects, such as a rabbit's foot, that are supposed to have special powers?

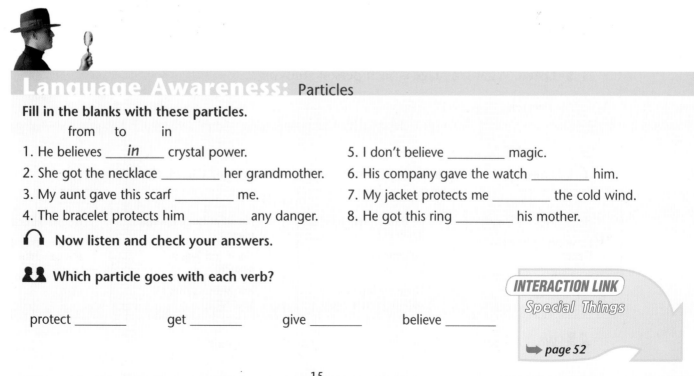

Language Awareness: Particles

Fill in the blanks with these particles.

        from   to   in

1. He believes ___*in*___ crystal power.

2. She got the necklace _____ her grandmother.

3. My aunt gave this scarf _____ me.

4. The bracelet protects him _____ any danger.

5. I don't believe _____ magic.

6. His company gave the watch _____ him.

7. My jacket protects me _____ the cold wind.

8. He got this ring _____ his mother.

🎧 **Now listen and check your answers.**

👥 **Which particle goes with each verb?**

protect _____   get _____   give _____   believe _____

INTERACTION LINK
Special Things

➡ *page 52*

It changed my life

■ Vocabulary Task

Name the countries. What languages are spoken there?
Write a country or a language in the box.

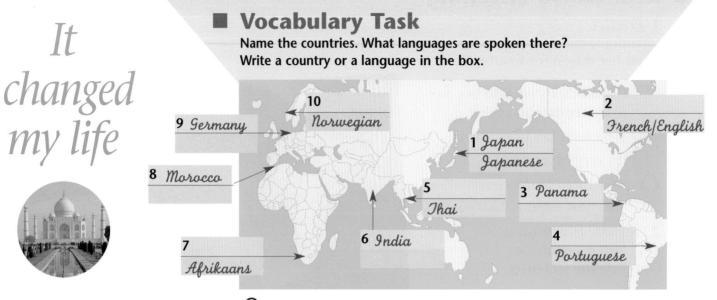

9 Germany

10 [   ] Norwegian

2 [   ] French/English

1 Japan [   ] Japanese

8 Morocco [   ]

5 [   ] Thai

3 Panama [   ]

6 India [   ]

4 [   ] Portuguese

7 [   ] Afrikaans

🎧 Now listen and check.

👥 Point to other countries on the map. Ask your partner to name the
country and the language.

■ Listening Task 👁 Why do you think these people are studying another language?

1 First Listening

🎧 Listen. What language is each person studying?

1. language
   French

2. language

3. language

4. language

2 Second Listening

🎧 Listen again. Why is each person studying a language? Check the reasons.

1.	2.	3.	4.
☑ His relatives are French.	☐ It's the best language in the world.	☐ No other language was offered.	☐ It's a challenge.
☑ He wants to travel to France.	☐ He's interested in business.	☐ Her friend lives in Mexico.	☐ It's the hardest language she can think of.
☐ His relatives don't speak any English.	☐ There are business opportunities in Japan.	☐ Her friends speak Spanish.	☐ She knew she couldn't do it.

👥 What are some good reasons for studying another language?

■ Real World Listening

1 Predict

Dave is studying Thai. What do you think he says about it?

__ It's hard to find materials.
__ It has different tones.
__ It's difficult to learn.
__ The writing system is different.
__ His friends laugh at him.
__ Thai people help him learn the language.

🎧 **Now listen and check your predictions.**

2 Get the main ideas

🎧 **Listen again. Write** T **(True),** F **(False),**
or ? **(I don't know) for each statement.**

__ 1. Dave lives in Thailand.
__ 2. Dave had a good experience in Thailand.
__ 3. Dave likes writing Thai.
__ 4. Thailand is "The Land of Laughs."
__ 5. People in Thailand laugh at him when he makes a mistake.
__ 6. Thai is easy to learn.

3 Respond to the ideas

Dave says, "You've just got to get into it."
What do you think he means?
Do you feel the same way about English? Why or why not?

Language Awareness: Reasons

Fill in each blank. Use:

> so   so that   in order to   that's why   because   because of

1. I want to study Japanese ___*because*___ it's the language of my ancestors.

2. I hope to learn a little Thai _____ I can speak to people next time I visit Thailand.

3. I'm learning English _____ get a job in the States.

4. Why is Chinese so difficult for me to learn? Maybe it's _____ the writing system.

5. I wanted to study a language that's different from English, _____ I chose Russian.

6. Why am I studying French? I have some relatives in France and I'd like to visit them someday. _____ .

🎧 **Now listen and check your answers.**

👥 **How can you say each sentence another way?**
Example: Japanese is the language of my ancestors. That's why I want to study it.

INTERACTION LINK
English Survey

➡ *page 53*

What do you like about him?

■ Vocabulary Task

Think of one of your good friends. Check the words that describe him or her.

☐ outgoing   ☐ shy   ☐ talkative   ☐ sense of humor
☐ sensitive   ☐ selfish   ☐ odd   ☐ honest
☐ funny   ☐ sweet   ☐ serious

🎧 **Now listen to these descriptions. Fill in the missing words.**

1. Steve is great! He's _____*sweet*_____ and he has a good _____.
2. I like people who are _____ , because I like to laugh. I don't care for people who are too _____.
3. Sure, Jana is very _____; it's too bad she's also kind of _____.
4. Brad is a little _____ , but I like that he's so _____ and _____.
5. Cindy is so cute! I just love how _____ and _____ she is.

👥 **Which of the words have a positive meaning? Which have a negative meaning? Can any have both a positive and negative meaning?**

■ Listening Task 👁 Look at the pictures. What do you think these people are like?

1 First Listening

🎧 Listen. Some people are talking about the kinds of people they like. What qualities does each person like?

Lisa

Mark

Stuart

Francine

1. quality they like
honest/humor
2. quality they like
3. quality they like
4. quality they like

2 Second Listening

🎧 Listen again. What quality does each person NOT like?

1. quality they don't like
selfish
2. quality they don't like
3. quality they don't like
4. quality they don't like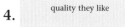

👥 Ask your partner: What qualities do you look for in a friend?

■ Real World Listening

1 Predict

Sheri is telling her co-worker about a new guy she met. **What do you think she likes about him?**

☐ He's serious.   ☐ He's funny.   ☐ He's handsome.

☐ He's sensitive.   ☐ He wears nice clothes.

🎧 Now listen and check your prediction.

2 Get the main ideas

🎧 Listen again. Answer the questions.

1. Where did Sheri go on her date?
2. What did the man do that surprised Sheri?
3. How did she react?
4. How does Jeremy react to this story?

3 Respond to the ideas

Sheri thinks that sensitivity is important in a relationship. Do you agree? What's important to you?

Language Awareness: Nouns and Adjectives

Choose a word for each blank.

athletic   witty   simple   crazy   casual   differences   good looks

1. He's got a ____crazy____ side to him. I actually like his craziness.
2. Those two are very different. I think they enjoy their _____ .
3. She's really _____ . I didn't think I'd ever want to date an athlete, but she's nice.
4. You're actually a _____ person. I think simplicity is a great quality.
5. He's so _____ . I love his sense of humor. He makes everyone laugh.
6. He's very _____ about his dress and way of talking. I don't like people who are too formal.
7. My sister is _____ about music. We go to a lot of concerts together.
8. He's very good-looking. I admit, I'm attracted to his _____ .

🎧 Now listen and check your answers.

👥 How are words such as *athlete* and *athletic* similar? How are they used differently in the sentences above?

INTERACTION LINK
A Perfect Match
➡ page 54

I really take after my Dad

■ Vocabulary Task

Read the sentences about families. Who are they talking about? Write a word that has the same meaning as the bold words.

cousins	brother-in-law	adopted	nephews
half-sisters	stepmother	niece	

1. My **brother's daughter** (*niece*) is so cute. She's only two but she can sing 10 songs.

2. I get along OK with my **Dad's new wife** (   ). She's actually pretty nice.

3. When I was little, I used to go to camp with my **uncle and aunt's children** (   ). They were like my brothers and sisters.

4. Everybody had a great time at my sister's wedding. My **sister's new husband** (   ) was even dancing on the tables.

5. After my mother remarried, she and Robert had two **girls** (*my*   ). But we feel like one family and I call them my sisters.

6. I'm not in a hurry to have kids yet. I spend a lot of time with my **brother's three boys** (   ) and I know they can be a handful.

7. We are so happy to have Lena. We **made her our legal child** (*her*) when she was just three months old.

🎧 **Now listen and check your answers.**

👥 **Ask your partner to close his or her book. See if your partner remembers the words.** Example: *What do you call your sister's husband?*

■ Listening Task ◉ Look at the picture. What do you think the relationships are between these people?

1 First Listening

🎧 **Listen. Steve is talking about the picture of his family.**
Write the relationship for each person.

Steve

2. Tara _____

4. _____

3. Jake _____

1. Angie _____

1. _____ father _____

4. Cristina _____

2 Second Listening

🎧 **Listen again. Match the people with what Steve says about them.**

Tara	a. Looks like Steve's father
Jake	b. Was adopted
His mother	c. Likes to read and play piano
Cristina	d. Lives in California

👥 **Tell a partner about your own family.**

■ **Real World Listening**

1 Predict

This is Jane, with her mother and father.
What do you think she has in common with her mother? **Write an** M.
What do you think she has in common with her father? **Write an** F.

   ___ likes the outdoors   ___ enjoys gardening   ___ likes snowboarding
   ___ has beautiful eyes   ___ enjoys dangerous activities   ___ has a trim figure
   ___ loves surfing   ___ is very intelligent

  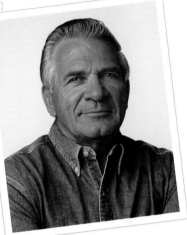

   Now listen to the conversation.

2 Get the main ideas

   Listen again. Complete the sentences.

1. Jane looks like her _____. They both _____.
2. Jane acts like her _____. They both _____.
3. Jane is proud that she takes after her _____.

3 Respond to the ideas

Who do you take after? In what ways?
Are there some similarities between you and your parents that you don't like?

Language Awareness: Response phrases

Match the statement with a response.

1. My mother has brown hair.   ___ a. And so am I.
2. My brother is in high school.   ___ b. Neither do I.
3. Jason can skateboard.   ___ c. I do, too.
4. Jim loves to go to the movies.   ___ d. Neither does mine.
5. Your family is small.   ___ e. And so is mine.
6. He doesn't have a sister.   ___ f. And so can I.
7. Her father doesn't snowboard. _1_ g. And so do I.

   Now listen and check your answers.

   How do you decide which verb to use in the rejoinder?

INTERACTION LINK
Something in Common

➡ *page 55*

Where the heck am I ?

■ Vocabulary Task

Complete the directions.

across	down	go along	until you get to
go down	go to	on your left	get to
take a taxi	turn right		

1. _Go to_ the end of this hallway. It's the last door _____ .

2. Marla's house? _____ this street. Her place is _____ the bridge.

3. Drive _____ Spring Street about half a mile. _____ at University.

4. Walk until you _____ the river. Then _____ the river _____ the tower.

5. The Hard Rock Café is very hard to find. You'd better _____ .

🎧 **Now listen and check your answers.**

👥 **Think of a place in the building you are in. Give your partner directions to get there. Have them guess where they are going.**

■ Listening Task 👁 Start at the ✘. Give directions to three places on the map.

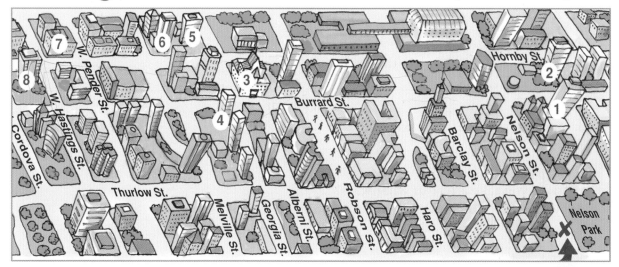

1 First Listening

🎧 **Listen. Four travelers in Vancouver are looking for their hotels.**
All of them are starting at Nelson Park. Write the number for each hotel.

1. _3_ Hotel Vancouver   2. ___ Century Plaza   3. ___ Hyatt Regency   4. ___ Days Inn

2 Second Listening

🎧 **Listen again. What directions do they give? Check the sentences.**

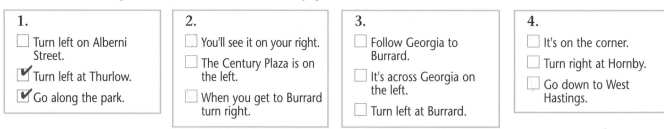

1.	2.	3.	4.
☐ Turn left on Alberni Street.	☐ You'll see it on your right.	☐ Follow Georgia to Burrard.	☐ It's on the corner.
☑ Turn left at Thurlow.	☐ The Century Plaza is on the left.	☐ It's across Georgia on the left.	☐ Turn right at Hornby.
☑ Go along the park.	☐ When you get to Burrard turn right.	☐ Turn left at Burrard.	☐ Go down to West Hastings.

👥 **Have you ever gotten lost because of bad directions? Tell your partner what happened.**

■ Real World Listening

1 Predict

Paula is talking about her visit to Turkey. What do you think happened?

☐ She forgot her money.

☐ She tried to speak Turkish but no one understood her.

☐ She got lost.

☑ She saw something scary.

🎧 **Now listen to her story.**

2 Get the main ideas

🎧 **Listen again. Answer the questions.**

1. Why did Paula go out alone?
2. Who helped Paula?
3. Where did he take her?
4. How did Paula feel?
5. What happened after they arrived?

3 Respond to the ideas

Paula says she decided not to be afraid to take chances when she's traveling in a new place. Do you think this is a wise idea for a woman?

Would you give a man the same advice? Why or why not?

Language Awareness: Paraphrasing

Look at the following directions. Say them in the shortest way you can.

Example: *Go down Nelson Street until you get to Burrard Street. When you get to Burrard turn right. You'll see the Century Plaza on your right.*

Shorter: ***Take Nelson to Burrard, turn right and the Century Plaza is on the right.***

1. Go along the park until you get to Thurlow Street. Turn left at Thurlow. Walk until you get to Alberni Street. Turn right on Alberni and go one block. Hotel Vancouver is at the end of the street.

2. Go back down Nelson and turn left at Burrard. Follow Burrard until you get to Georgia. The Hyatt Regency is across Georgia on the far left corner.

🎧 **Now listen and check.**

👥 **What information is the most important in giving directions?**
Underline the most important information above.

INTERACTION LINK
Hide & Seek

➡ *page 56*

You can meet lots of important people

■ Vocabulary Task

Read about these jobs. What is the main feature of each person's job? Write the word in the space.

responsibility	flexible schedule	prestige
travel	long hours	teamwork
high pay	telecommuting	

travel   1. I'm a tour guide. I get to see a lot of exotic places all over the world.

_____ 2. I'm a teacher. I like my job because I feel that, in a way, the future of my students is in my hands.

_____ 3. I'm a flight attendant. I only have to work three days a week.

_____ 4. As a journalist, I get to meet a lot of important people.

_____ 5. I'm a stockbroker. My job is stressful, but I'll be able to retire by the time I'm 40!

_____ 6. I'm a nurse. I love helping people get better, but sometimes I don't get home until late at night.

_____ 7. I love being a firefighter. My co-workers and I really count on each other during a fire.

_____ 8. I'm a computer programmer. My company allows me to work from my computer at home.

🎧 **Now listen and check.**

👥 **Which of the jobs above would you like? Why? Which feature is most important to you?**

■ Listening Task 👁 Look at the pictures. What do you think each person's job is?

1 First Listening

🎧 **Listen. Where did each speaker work?**

1. an accessories shop   2. _____   3. _____   4. _____

2 Second Listening

🎧 **Listen again. Why was the job a good experience for the speaker? Check the main reason.**

1. Leslie	2. Arthur	3. Nima	4. Anna
☐ had a good schedule	☐ learned to work quickly	☐ it was easy	☐ had many chances to ski
☑ could practice foreign languages	☐ learned to use a cash register	☐ learned to work on computers	☐ saw beautiful scenery

👥 **If you've had a job, what was your first job like? If not, what would you like your first job to be?**

■ Real World Listening

1 Predict
Here are some things that Amy likes:
meeting people   travel   writing e-mail   reading   living in other countries   interesting events
What do you think Amy's ideal job is?

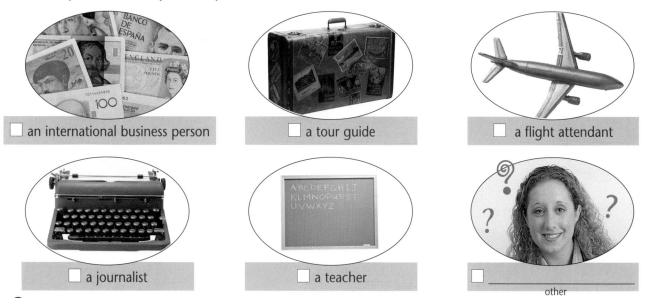

| □ an international business person | □ a tour guide | □ a flight attendant |

| □ a journalist | □ a teacher | □ _____ other |

🎧 **Now listen and check your prediction.**

2 Get the main ideas
🎧 **Listen again. Answer the questions.**

1. Why did Amy apply for this job?
2. What did the interviewer ask about?
3. What are Amy's strong points for this job?
4. What are Amy's weak points?

3 Respond to the ideas
Do you think Amy will get this job? Why or why not? What is your ideal job?

Language Awareness: Talking about the past

🎧 **Listen. Complete each sentence.**

1. _____*I used to work*_____ in a clothing shop.
2. _____ work 50 hours at the restaurant.
3. _____ all day in front of a computer.
4. _____ a journalist.
5. _____ as a maid in a tourist hotel.
6. _____ as a flight attendant.

👥 **Which sentences are in the past?**
What are some ways to show one is talking about the past?

INTERACTION LINK
Job Search
➡ *page 57*

We have a few rules

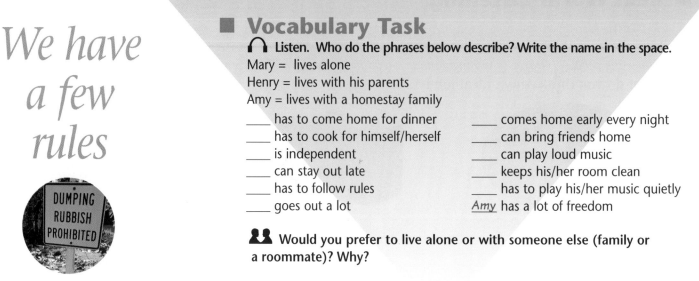

DUMPING RUBBISH PROHIBITED

■ Vocabulary Task

🎧 **Listen.** Who do the phrases below describe? Write the name in the space.

Mary = lives alone
Henry = lives with his parents
Amy = lives with a homestay family

____ has to come home for dinner
____ has to cook for himself/herself
____ is independent
____ can stay out late
____ has to follow rules
____ goes out a lot

____ comes home early every night
____ can bring friends home
____ can play loud music
____ keeps his/her room clean
____ has to play his/her music quietly
Amy has a lot of freedom

👥 Would you prefer to live alone or with someone else (family or a roommate)? Why?

■ Listening Task 👁 What kind of living situation does each picture show?

John   **Susan**   **Eli**   **Tracy**

1 First Listening

🎧 Listen. Some people are talking about their living situations. What bothers them about where they live?

1.
☐ Doesn't like mom's cooking
☐ Has to cook
☑ Parents' schedule

2.
☐ Can't go shopping
☐ Not used to rules
☐ Can't have visitors

3.
☐ Hard to get a lot of sleep
☐ Must eat in cafeteria
☐ Can't stay out late

4.
☐ Can't choose schedule
☐ Has to clean and do laundry
☐ Room is always dirty

2 Second Listening

🎧 Listen again. What is one thing the speaker appreciates about their living situation?

1. _mom's cooking_   2. _____   3. _____   4. _____

👥 Where do you live? What do you appreciate about it? What bothers you about it?

■ Real World Listening

1 *Predict*

What do people usually do on a vacation?

___ sleep late

___ eat good food

___ go sightseeing

___ stay in nice hotels

___ watch television

___ read books

___ go shopping

___ go hiking

🎧 Now listen to the conversation. What things will Cathy and Kevin do on their vacation?

2 *Get the main ideas*

🎧 Listen again. Look at the brochure for Camp Star. Correct the five mistakes.

CAMP ★ STAR

This week's program:
- Hiking
- Lectures
- Computer Class

Camp Star is on Star Island.

You must come to the island by train.

Guests stay in tents.

Camp Star Rules
1. No using telephones (except in emergency).
2. No reading books.
3. Everyone must wake up early and go hiking.
4. No television after 10:00 PM.

3 *Respond to the ideas*

Do you think Kevin and Cathy will go to Camp Star? Why or why not?
Would you go to Camp Star? Why or why not?

Language Awareness: Modals

Complete each sentence with the correct modal.

can   can't   have to   don't have to

1. We ___*can't*___ have pets in the dorm. I really miss my dog. I wish I could play my music loud, too. But I _____ — it's a dorm rule. And if somebody comes to visit me, I _____ meet them in the lounge. No visitors in the room.

2. At my parents' house, I _____ come home by 11:00 or else they worry about me. It's not so bad, though. I _____ help around the house because my parents do all the housework. I'm going to stay here until I _____ afford to live on my own.

🎧 **Now listen and check your answers.**

👥 Which of the modals means *must*? *Must not*?
Which of the modals show there is a choice?

INTERACTION LINK

A Great Place to Visit

➡ *page 58*

They lost my luggage!

■ Vocabulary Task

Choose the correct words to complete the sentences.

baggage claim	luggage	carry-on	visa
replacement	window seats	wrong line	economy
flight	passport		

1. Your attention, please. __*Flight*__ 275 to Miami will be delayed for two hours.
2. I'm sorry, there are no _____ left. Would you like an aisle seat?
3. Uh-oh, I think I left my _____ bag on the plane.
4. Your _____ has expired. You can't leave the country.
5. Aagh! I waited for over an hour in the _____!
6. Excuse me. I left my ticket at home. Can I get a _____ ?
7. My suitcase is not here at the _____.
8. I'm sorry, all our _____ seats are sold out. How about business class?
9. Too much _____? But I only have three suitcases.
10. You'll need a tourist _____ to enter the country.

🎧 **Listen and check your answers.**

👥 **Ask your partner: What do you like about traveling? What do you dislike?**

■ Listening Task 👁 Look at the pictures. What problem do you think each traveler has?

1 First Listening

🎧 **What is the problem?**

1. ☑ forgot passport   2. ☐ wrong line   3. ☐ flight is sold out   4. ☐ lost luggage
   ☐ forgot ticket   ☐ wrong airline   ☐ flight is canceled   ☐ luggage damaged

2 Second Listening

🎧 **What will happen next?**

1.	2.	3.	4.
☐ He will go back home. ☑ He will call Susan.	☐ The flight will be delayed. ☐ She will wait for 30 minutes.	☐ He will leave tomorrow morning. ☐ He will fly first class.	☐ He will have his bags delivered. ☐ He will wait for his bags.

👥 **What are some other problems that travelers might have?**

■ Real World Listening

1 Predict

Trevor went to Costa Rica. What do you think happened? Fill in the blanks in his postcard.

🎧 Now listen and check your guesses.

2 Get the main ideas

🎧 Listen again. What were his problems? Check *a* or *b* for each problem.

1st problem:
☐ a. His passport was expired.
☐ b. He forgot his passport.

2nd problem:
☐ a. He missed his flight.
☐ b. His flight was canceled.

3rd problem:
☐ a. The airport was closed.
☐ b. The plane needed repairs.

4th problem:
☐ a. His luggage was lost.
☐ b. The airline clerk ignored him.

3 Respond to the ideas

Do you think Trevor was sorry he took this trip? Why or why not?
Have you ever had a similar experience?

Dave,
You'll never believe how my trip has been. First, I _____ my passport! That was bad enough, but then I _____ my flight. After I finally took off, we had _____ trouble and had to _____ in Mexico City. I was stuck in Mexico City for almost a whole _____! When I finally got to Costa Rica, my _____ was missing. It seemed like a horrible trip, but then it all changed.

Trevor

Dave Simmone
3341 Creeland
Cupertino

Greetings from Beautiful Costa R

Language Awareness: Reduced Forms

🎧 **Listen and underline the reduced words.**

1. I <u>have to</u> be at a business meeting in Dallas tomorrow.

2. We're going to fly first class this time.

3. You should have packed your bags last night.

4. It's kind of late to change plans now.

5. Aren't you going to check in first?

6. I'm kind of excited about going to China.

7. We've got to be ready to leave by 6:30.

8. John's going to call me from the airport.

9. You don't have to leave now, do you?

10. You've got to get a visa first.

🎧 **Now listen and check your answers.**

👥 How are the reduced forms pronounced in daily conversation? For example, *kind of* sounds like *kinda*.

INTERACTION LINK
The Terrible Trip Game
➡ *page 59*

Check this out!

■ Vocabulary Task

Match the questions with the correct answers.

1. Is this your new **modem**?
2. How much did that **laser printer** cost?
3. So this is a **zip drive**, huh?
4. Wow! Is that your new **scanner**?
5. What does the **mouse** do?
6. What kind of **software** do you have?
7. Why do they call it a **notebook**?
8. What kind of **disks** can this computer read?
9. What size **monitor** should I buy?

a. Yeah. I can store up to 100 megabytes of data with it.

b. It wasn't too expensive, and it prints out high-quality copies

c. Yes. It lets me hook up to the Internet at 128 kilobytes per second.

d. I have a graphics program, a word processing program, and an e-mail program.

e. Uh-huh. Check out these pictures I scanned for my website.

f. It lets you move the pointer around the screen and click on things.

g. The bigger it is, the more you can see on the screen.

h. Because it's so small it can fit in your bag.

i. It'll read DVDs and CD-ROMs.

🎧 Listen and check your answers.

👥 Do you have any of these items? Which ones would you like to have? Why?

■ Listening Task 👁 What are these items? How do you use them?

1 First Listening

🎧 Listen. Which of the items does the speaker have?

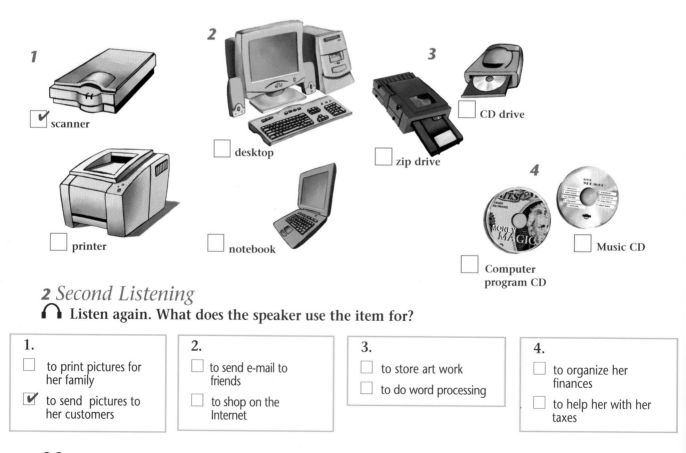

1
☑ scanner
☐ printer

2
☐ desktop
☐ notebook

3
☐ zip drive
☐ CD drive

4
☐ Computer program CD
☐ Music CD

2 Second Listening

🎧 Listen again. What does the speaker use the item for?

1.	2.	3.	4.
☐ to print pictures for her family	☐ to send e-mail to friends	☐ to store art work	☐ to organize her finances
☑ to send pictures to her customers	☐ to shop on the Internet	☐ to do word processing	☐ to help her with her taxes

👥 Which machines do you use most at your work or school?

■ Real World Listening

1 Predict

Leon has started an Internet business called DivineDVDs.com. What do you think his business sells?

☐ video cassettes ☐ movies on DVDs ☐ game software ☐ other?

∩ Now listen and check your prediction.

2 Get the main ideas

∩ Listen again. What does Leon use these things for?

scanner   DVD player
headset   cardboard boxes

3 Respond to the ideas

Do you think Leon's business will be successful?
Leon says that to work from home you have to be disciplined.
What are some problems you might have if you worked from home?
What do you think you would miss about working in an office or a place with other workers?

Language Awareness: Two-Part Verbs

Fill in the missing part of the two-part verbs.

in   up   out   on   to   down

1. He will scan __in__ the pictures to ____-load_ to his homepage.

2. Please _____ load the file from the server.

3. He typed _____ the data to his laptop computer.

4. The modem allows you to connect _____ the Internet.

5. Let's hook _____ our new DVD drive.

6. Don't forget to print _____ the order.

7. She can log _____ to the Internet from anywhere with her cellular phone.

8. He plugs _____ a headset when he answers the phone.

∩ Now listen and check your answers.

👥 What English computer words are used in your language?

INTERACTION LINK
Internet Business
➡ *page 60*

I can squeeze you in...

■ Vocabulary Task

Sheila is trying to schedule a meeting with Tom. Complete the conversation.

full	squeeze it in	free
busy	impossible	light
open	tight	booked

Sheila: Tom, I can't make that meeting on Tuesday. My schedule is pretty _____ *full* _____ . Tuesday is _____ .

Tom: Yeah. Looks like you'll be too _____ . You're _____ solid all day. Can you make it Monday?

Sheila: I might be able to _____ at 10:00. It'll be _____ though.

Tom: How's Wednesday? Do you have any _____ time?

Sheila: Wednesday's schedule is pretty _____ . After 10:00 I'm _____ .

Tom: OK, let's try for 11:00 on Wednesday.

🎧 **Listen and check your answers.**

👥 **What is your schedule like for this week? Are there any times you and your partner are both free? Who has a busier schedule?**

■ Listening Task 👁 Look at Steve's schedule. What is he going to do each day?

1 First Listening
🎧 **Listen. What is Steve going to do?**

1. ☑ watch his children
   ☐ go to the gym

2. ☐ have dinner with Sandy
   ☐ see a movie with Sandy

3. ☐ have a drink with Bob
   ☐ see a baseball game with Bob

4. ☐ take care of Larry's dog
   ☐ go to work

2 Second Listening
🎧 **Listen again. Complete Steve's schedule.**

Thursday	Friday	Saturday	Sunday
5:00 -	5:00 -	5:00 -	12:00 -
6:00 -	6:00 -	6:00 -	1:00 -
7:00 -	7:00 -	7:00 -	2:00 -
8:00 -	8:00 -	8:00 -	3:00 -
9:00 -	9:00 -	9:00 -	4:00 -
10:00 -	10:00 -	10:00 -	

👥 **Tell your partner your schedule for this coming weekend.**

■ **Real World Listening**

1 Predict

Meet Pink!, a very busy all-woman rock band.
Check the items you think might be on their schedule.

☐ go to an autograph signing session   ☐ take music lessons

☐ play at the Rock and Roll Hall of Fame   ☐ record a new CD

☐ go to church   ☐ do a live online chat on MTV.com

🎧 **Now listen and check your predictions.**

2 Get the main ideas

🎧 **Listen again. What events does Pink! have to attend? Complete the list.**

- _____ in Middleburg.
- _____ in Cleveland.
- _____ in Akron.
- _____ in Pittsburgh.
- _____ in St. Louis.

3 Respond to the ideas

Do you think the band is successful? Do you think this is a typical lifestyle for a rock band?

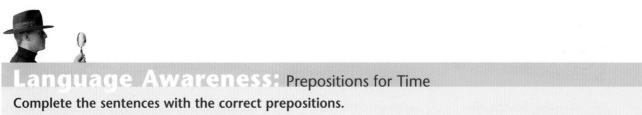

Language Awareness: Prepositions for Time

Complete the sentences with the correct prepositions.

     at   between   from   in

1. I have an important meeting ___*at*___ 3:00 PM.

2. The concert is _____ 6:30 to 8:00.

3. Let's hurry. The movie starts _____ 10 minutes.

4. He is free _____ 2:00 and 3:00 today.

5. Tell him I'll get back to him _____ a few days.

6. You must get there early because the doors close _____ 1:30.

7. The event runs _____ Monday to Friday next week.

8. I have a lot to do _____ now and then.

🎧 **Now listen and check your answers.**

👥 When do you use *from* and *between*?
When do you use *in* and *at*?

INTERACTION LINK
Making Plans

➡ *page 61*

33

It was a real scorcher!

■ Vocabulary Task

When would you usually use these words? Write them under the season.

blizzard	showers	scorching	muggy
chilly	thunder	humid	flurries
freezing	lightning	damp	rainy
	overcast	breezy	

Spring	Summer	Fall	Winter
breezy *damp* *showers*			

🎧 Listen and check your answers.

👥 What other words can you add to the chart?

■ Listening Task ◉ Describe the weather in each picture. What season do you think it is?

1 First Listening

🎧 It's New Year's Day. Listen to world weather reports for four different cities. Write one word the reporter uses to describe the weather.

| Auckland, New Zealand | San Diego, California | San Jose, Costa Rica | Edmonton, Alberta |

1. scorching 2. 3. 4.

2 Second Listening

🎧 Listen again. What activity does each reporter suggest doing for the day?

1. beach 2. 3. 4.

👥 What's the weather usually like on New Year's Day where you live? Do you like it?

■ **Real World Listening**

1 Predict

Lena is looking at some photos of Alaska with her grandson Alex. **What do you think she will talk about?**

○ camping	○ fishing	○ blizzards	○ skiing	○ buffalo
○ bears	○ swimming	○ wolves	○ snowmen	○ puppies

🎧 **Now listen to the conversation.**

2 Get the main ideas

🎧 **Listen again.** What does she say about each season?

winter   spring

summer   fall

3 Respond to the ideas

Lena talks about childhood memories of different seasons. What special memories do you have of the seasons?

Language Awareness: Weather Idioms

Match each idiom with its meaning.

WEATHER IDIOMS

f 1. Save for a rainy day.

___ 2. Every cloud has a silver lining.

___ 3. He's a fair-weather friend.

___ 4. You'll have to take a rain check on that item.

___ 5. She has her head in the clouds.

___ 6. It's raining cats and dogs.

___ 7. He's feeling under the weather.

___ 8. I am snowed under with work.

MEANING

a. *When you're having a bad time, this friend will not be there to help you.*

b. *Bad things always have a good side.*

c. *He's not well or is depressed (feeling sad).*

d. *I have too much work to do.*

e. *It's a very heavy rainstorm.*

f. *Keep to use later.*

g. *That item is not available now.*

h. *She can't think about everyday matters.*

🎧 **Now listen and check your answers.**

👥 Why do you think there are so many idioms related to weather?

INTERACTION LINK

The Four Seasons Game

➡ *page s 63-65*

I couldn't say no...

■ Vocabulary Task

Match the invitations and the responses.

Invitations

1. Want to come over for dinner tonight?

2. I'd appreciate it if you would call me back to let me know by this Friday.

3. Do you want to come to the mall with me?

4. Hey, it's John's birthday. "Join us for a party at 2:30 p.m. on April 1st."

5. It's an invitation. It says: We would like to request the pleasure of your company at eight o'clock on Thursday evening. Please RSVP to 555-1212.

6. Can you go to the movies with me?

7. Please come to a barbecue this Saturday at 1:00 p.m. BYOB.

Responses

a. *The first? I'll be out of town. I guess I better call to let them know.*

b. *I think I'm going to have to take a rain check. I have too much work to do this weekend.*

c. *It sounds like fun, but I'm really busy tonight.*

d. *I'd love to go. I'll call to RSVP.*

e. *Sure, I'd love to! What movie do you want to see?*

f. *I can let you know now. It would be my pleasure to attend.*

g. *Right now? OK. Just let me get my purse.*

🎧 Listen and check your answers.

👥 Which invitations and responses are formal? Which ones are casual?

■ Listening Task 💿 Look at the situations. Somebody is making an invitation. Which do you think are formal? Which do you think are casual?

1 First Listening
🎧 Listen. What is the invitation for?

1. banquet for Ms. Green   2.   3.   4.

2 Second Listening
🎧 Listen again. Is the invitation accepted or refused?

1. accepted   2.   3.   4.

👥 Which invitations are formal? Which are casual? How do you know?

■ **Real World Listening**

1 Predict

Katherine just started working at a small company.
She has a problem.
What do you think her problem is?

☐ She doesn't know anyone.

☐ She doesn't know how to do her job.

☐ Her boss keeps inviting her to go places.

☐ She has to wear a uniform.

☐ Her co-workers aren't very friendly.

🎧 **Now listen and check your prediction.**

2 Get the main ideas

🎧 **Listen again. Answer the questions.**
What invitations did Katherine accept?

Why?
What is she worried about now?

3 Respond to the ideas

Katherine asks, "How do I get out of this situation?" What advice would you give her?
Have you ever been invited to an event you didn't want to attend? What happened?

Language Awareness: Refusals

What do you think is a polite way to refuse an invitation? Rate the refusals.

P= *polite*   **NP**= *not polite*   **?**= *I'm not sure*

_P_ 1. It sounds like fun, but I'm really busy.   ___ 5. Nope. Can't make it.

___ 2. I'm sorry, I can't make it.   ___ 6. Sorry, not interested.

___ 3. I don't want to go.   ___ 7. I'm sorry, I have other plans. Can I take a rain check?

___ 4. No way.   ___ 8. Let me check my schedule.

🎧 **Now listen and check your answers.**

👥 **What do you think makes a refusal polite?**

___ showing you have no desire to attend   ___ offering to accept at another time

___ saying you are willing to go   ___ showing dislike of the activity

___ using short phrases   ___ simply refusing to attend

___ saying you have other plans   ___ using full sentences

Are these characteristics the same in your language?

INTERACTION LINK
Let's Party

➥ *page 66*

It's just like living on Earth

■ Vocabulary Task

Which of the following are important to you? Which are not so important? Rank the items from 1 (very important) to 10 (not so important).

___ public transportation   ___ movie theaters   ___ an airport
___ wide-open spaces   ___ hiking trails   ___ lots of parking
___ grass and trees   ___ convenience stores   ___ a library
___ shopping malls

Listen to the speakers.
What do they like about the areas they live in?

1. _a lot of shops..._____

2. _____

3. _____

Compare your rankings with your partner's. What kind of area do you think is best for you? Your partner?

■ Listening Task ◉ What kind of area do you live in? Is it urban, suburban, or rural?

1 First Listening

Listen. What kind of area does each speaker live in? Write *urban*, *suburban*, or *rural* under the picture.

1.   *suburban*   2.   3.   4.

2 Second Listening

Listen again. Write one thing the speaker appreciates.

1.   2.   3.   4.

What are some things you like about where you live? Is there anything you don't like?

■ Real World Listening

1 Predict

It's the middle of the 21st Century.
Julie lives on the international space
station. She is being interviewed by
a reporter. **What things do you think
you can find on the space station?**

☐ shopping malls   ☐ movie theaters

☐ mountains   ☐ airports

☐ wide-open spaces   ☐ public transportation

🎧 **Listen and check your predictions.**

2 Get the main ideas

🎧 **Listen again. Answer the questions.**

1. What does Julie say about these topics?

   • modern conveniences

   • food

   • nature

   • transportation

   • entertainment and work

   • what she dislikes

2. According to Julie, what are the advantages and disadvantages of living in the space station?

3 Respond to the ideas

Julie says, "It's really an ideal world." If you could live in an ideal world, what would it be like?

Language Awareness: Quantity Words

Complete this table.
Write the quantity words in the chart.

a lot/lots of   *a little*   *a few*   *some*   *not many*   *not much*

oranges	coffee	time	friends
a lot of			

🎧 **Now listen and check your answers.**

👥 **What is the difference between the nouns *oranges* and *coffee*?**

INTERACTION LINK
Space Station

➡ *page 67*

Unit **17**

I'll try anything!

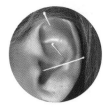

■ Vocabulary Task

Write *S* for symptom (the way you know something is wrong) or *T* for treatment (the way to make yourself better).

T 1. drink herbal tea/medicine
___ have a sore throat
___ 2. get a Shiatsu massage
___ have sore muscles
___ 3. feel a little down
___ use aromatherapy

___ 4. use a home remedy
___ catch a cold
___ 5. have a headache
___ get acupuncture
___ 6. try a relaxation exercise
___ feel stressed

🎧 Now listen and check your answers.

👥 Have you tried any of the treatments listed above? What symptoms did you have?

■ Listening Task 👁 Look at the pictures.
What problem do you think each customer has?

1 First Listening
🎧 Anna works in a natural foods shop. Listen to the customers. What are their symptons?

1. Symptom	2. Symptom	3. Symptom	4. Symptom
no energy			

2 Second Listening
🎧 Listen again. What treatment does Anna recommend for each customer?

1. *aromatherapy oil*	2.	3.	4.

👥 When was the last time you were sick? What kind of treatment did you use? Do you prefer to use modern medicine or natural ways to treat your illness?

■ **Real World Listening**

1 Predict

You will experience a relaxation exercise.
Close your eyes and imagine a scene that
makes you feel relaxed. **What do you see?**

🎧 Now listen to the exercise.

2 Get the main ideas
🎧 Listen again.

What does the speaker ask you to imagine?

Were you able to relax? Why or why not?

3 Respond to the ideas
The speaker says that relaxing will help you to feel well and happy.
Do you agree with this?
What do you do to relieve your own stress?

Language Awareness: Talking about Illnesses

Fill in the blanks with these words.

| *have* | *feel* | *catch* | *get* | *come down with* | *suffer from* | *test positive for* |

Be sure to change the verb tense if necessary.

1. I _____*have*_____ a headache. Do you have any pain reliever?
2. Katie didn't want to _____ a cold, so she stayed inside during the snowstorm.
3. In the spring, I always _____ hay fever.
4. Tyler _____ sick from eating too much chocolate.
5. It sounds like you _____ a sore throat. Do you want something to drink?
6. Many of the workers _____ something after the meeting.
7. You seem really hot. Do you _____ feverish?
8. Unfortunately, he _____diabetes.

🎧 **Now listen and check your answers.**

👥 Some phrases are associated with a particular illness, such as *catch* and *a cold*.
What illnesses do you use *get* with? *have*? *catch*?

INTERACTION LINK
Home Remedies

➡ *page 68*

Shopping here is so exciting!

■ Vocabulary Task

Look at the list of words in the chart. Choose the correct category words.

groceries   furniture   hardware
toys   baked goods   clothing
toiletries   electronics   liquor

1. *clothing*			2.
shirt	computer	chair	deodorant
pants	Walkman	sofa	soap
sweater	television	table	shampoo
jacket	video camera	desk	toothpaste

3.		4.	5.	6.
milk	tools	doll	beer	bread
eggs	lumber	blocks	wine	cake
bread	lock	train set	whiskey	cookies
vegetables	key	model airplane	liqueur	bagels

🎧 Now listen and check your answers.

👥 Do you like shopping? What do you enjoy shopping for?

■ Listening Task 👁 Look at the pictures. What kinds of items are they shopping for?

1 First Listening

🎧 Listen. What kind of items are they shopping for?

1. bread...
2.
3.
4.

2 Second Listening

🎧 What do the speakers say about their shopping experience?

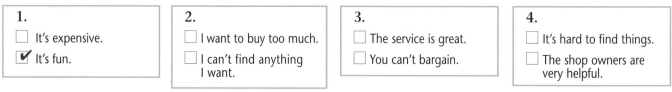

1.
☐ It's expensive.
☑ It's fun.

2.
☐ I want to buy too much.
☐ I can't find anything I want.

3.
☐ The service is great.
☐ You can't bargain.

4.
☐ It's hard to find things.
☐ The shop owners are very helpful.

👥 Where is your favorite place to shop? Tell your partner about it.

■ Real World Listening

1 Predict

Peggy takes her friend Amy shopping in a market in Africa.

What do you think Amy will learn about the market?

___ there are many languages spoken

___ the prices are high

___ you must bargain

___ the vendors come from a lot of different countries

___ other? _____

🎧 Now listen and check your prediction.

2 Get the main ideas

🎧 Listen again. Answer the questions.

1. What do Peggy and Amy want to buy?

2. What is new about shopping for Amy in this market?

3 Respond to the ideas

Amy says that shopping at this market is exciting.
Is shopping exciting for you? What makes it exciting?

Language Awareness: Money Idioms

Circle the idiom with the same meaning as the underlined word or phrase.

1. His children go to a private high school! The education is great but it costs him <u>a lot of money</u>.
   a. *an arm and a leg*   b. *money to burn*   c. *to bring home the bacon*

2. Let's all <u>contribute some money</u> to send the team to Europe.
   a. *hit pay dirt*   b. *rake in the money*   c. *chip in*

3. Many people are <u>making money from</u> investing in Internet businesses.
   a. *cashing in on*   b. *pinching pennies from*   c. *passing the buck on*

4. His family <u>doesn't have much money.</u>
   a. *is loaded*   b. *cleaned up*   c. *is hard up*

5. He is the CEO of a big company. He <u>gets paid a lot</u>.
   a. *rakes in the money*   b. *is stone broke*   c. *is a deadbeat*

6. My brother and I barely <u>gathered</u> enough money to pay our telephone bill.
   a. *cleaned up*   b. *kicked back*   c. *scraped together*

🎧 Now listen and check your answers.

👥 Which of these money idioms have a "good meaning"?
Which have a "bad meaning"?

INTERACTION LINK
Let's Make a Deal
➡ *page 69*

What'd you get?

■ Vocabulary Task

Fill in the missing words.

spicy	salty	sour	chewy
tastes	bland	raw	sweet

1. Yum! This chocolate is so ___sweet___ and creamy.

2. Nice face. Is that grapefruit too _____? Want some sugar for it?

3. Wow! This octopus isn't bad – kind of _____, though.

4. This is ostrich? It _____ like chicken.

5. You made this salsa? Mmm, _____. I like it.

6. Hmm. I think I like the shrimp better. The squid was kind of _____.

7. I'm thirsty. That popcorn was really _____.

8. Wait a second! Aren't you going to cook that first? You're not going to eat that _____, are you?

🎧 Now listen and check your answers.

👥 What is your favorite food? Why do you like it?

■ Listening Task 👁 Look at the soups. How do you think they taste?

1 First Listening

🎧 Listen. How does the waiter describe each soup?

1. Gazpacho
cold tomato soup with...

2. Split-pea soup

3. Pumpkin soup

4. Jambalaya

2 Second Listening

🎧 Listen again. Cross out the item that is NOT in each soup:

1.	2.	3.	4.
tomatoes, onions, celery, cucumber, lime juice	tomatoes, onions, celery, carrots, ham, peas	oats, pumpkin, cinnamon, nutmeg, brown sugar	sausage, tomatoes, shrimp, pepper, chili powder

👥 What's your favorite soup? What is in it?

■ **Real World Listening**

1 Predict

Jim and Sandy are eating lunch at an international food mall.
What do you think they will say about their food?

octopus

raw shrimp

ostrich burger

french fries

🎧 Now listen and check your prediction.

2 Get the main ideas

🎧 Listen again. What do they say about the food? Fill in the chart.

	Jim	Sandy
ostrich burger		
pizza/octopus		
shrimp		
french fries		

3 Respond to the ideas

Do you think the foods they mentioned are strange?
What's the strangest thing you've ever eaten?

Language Awareness: Food Idioms

Match the idiom with its meaning.

Idiom

1. Give it to me in a nutshell. I don't have much time. _f_
2. Let's chew the fat a while. ____
3. Don't cry over spilt milk. ____
4. It was a piece of cake. ____
5. You're full of beans tonight! ____
6. He's a bad egg. ____
7. You'd better take what she says with a grain of salt. ____
8. She's the apple of his eye. ____

Meaning

a. You can't change the past.
b. Don't believe everything she says.
c. You should avoid him — he's not a good person.
d. You're talking nonsense!
e. He loves her.
f. Tell me briefly, please.
g. It was very easy.
h. Let's talk.

🎧 Now listen and check your answers.

👥 What idioms about food do you have in your language?
How are they different from the ones you know in English?

INTERACTION LINK

*Try It—
You'll Like It*

➡ *page 71*

This just in...

■ Vocabulary Task

Fill in the blanks in each sentence.

teen pregnancy	violence	drug addiction
drinking age	modern families	gun laws
education	pressure	

1. *Teen pregnancy* is causing concern among doctors.

2. The mayor will promote stricter _____ to reduce crime.

3. Many _____ are single-parent households.

4. Experts say that crime among young people is caused by _____ in movies.

5. Teachers say more money is needed for _____ .

6. A famous rock star is being treated for _____ .

7. Children are under _____ to succeed at a young age.

8. The police are against lowering the _____ .

🎧 . **Now listen and check your answers.**

👥 **Ask your partner: Which of the issues in these headlines are problems in your own country?**

■ Listening Task 👁 Look at the headlines.
What do you think the news stories are about?

1 First Listening
🎧 Listen to each conversation. What issue do the speakers discuss?

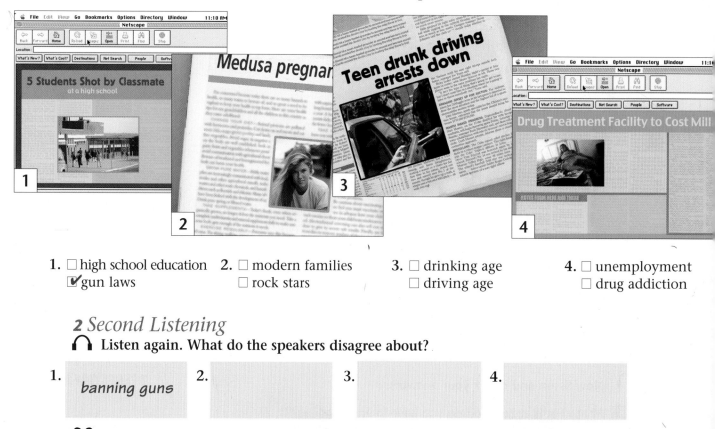

1. ☐ high school education
   ☑ gun laws

2. ☐ modern families
   ☐ rock stars

3. ☐ drinking age
   ☐ driving age

4. ☐ unemployment
   ☐ drug addiction

2 Second Listening
🎧 Listen again. What do the speakers disagree about?

1. banning guns   2. _____   3. _____   4. _____

👥 **How do you feel about these issues? Share your opinions with a classmate.**

■ Real World Listening

1 Predict

A psychology class is talking about a recent news story in their city. A young child ran away from home because his parents put too much pressure on him to do well in school.
What do you think some of the arguments on this topic will be?

So, I think parents should...

I'm glad that my parents...

I hear the same thing all the time...

Kids need their parents to...

∩ Now listen to the discussion.

2 Get the main ideas

∩ Listen again. **What is each student's opinion?**

Christina ☐ a. Kids should have less freedom.
☐ b. Parents should not pressure their kids.

Eric ☐ a. Kids need a little pressure to succeed.
☐ b. Kids will work hard without parents' pressure.

Julia ☐ a. Children should excel at what their parents like.
☐ b. Parents should encourage children to excel at something the children like.

3 Respond to the ideas

Which student do you agree with?
Were you pressured to learn at an early age?
How did you feel about it?

Language Awareness: Headlines

Explain what each headline means.

1. Government to Push for Longer Holidays.
   Example: *The government is going to try to make longer holidays.*

2. City Child Care Costs Cut _____

3. Euro Up Against Dollar _____

4. Lab Sees Animal Rights Protest _____

5. Jobs Rise in New Year _____

6. UN Plan Gets Third World Support _____

∩ **Now listen and check your answers.**

👥 What kinds of words are left out in headlines?

INTERACTION LINK

News Debate

➡ *page 73*

INTERACTION LINKS

Work with your classmates.
Do one activity after you finish each unit.

Meet the Class

Get to know your classmates!

Write information about yourself in the chart below.
Then walk around your class and introduce yourself to your classmates.
Ask questions. Find three people you have something in common with.
Fill their names in the chart.

TOPIC	Information about me	Classmate with the same answer
My favorite food		
My favorite movie		
Month I was born in		
Something I don't like		
My dream vacation		

Model Conversation 1:
Hideo introduces himself to Andrea.

    A: *Hi, I'm Hideo.*
    B: *Good to meet you. My name's Andrea.*
    A: *What's your favorite food?*
    B: *It's spaghetti. What's yours?*
    A: *Mine is spaghetti, too! I'll write your name on my chart. How do you spell it?*

Model Conversation 2:
Andrea introduces Mario to Hideo.

    A: *Hi, Mario. Have you met Hideo? Hideo, this is Mario.*
    B: *Not yet. Hi, Hideo. Hey, what month were you born in?*
    C: *July. How about you, Mario?*
    B: *September. Why don't you ask Paula? I think she was born in July.*
    C: *Thanks. Paula, when were you born?*

Get in Touch

Make a class list with the names, phone numbers and e-mail addresses of your classmates. Try to get information from at least 10 people.

	NAME	PHONE NUMBER	E-MAIL ADDRESS
1			
2			
3			
4			
5			
6			
7			
8			
9			
10			
11			
12			

Model Conversation 1:

Sirpa: *Hi, Junichi, I'm making a class contact list. Can you spell your name for me?*
Junichi: *Sure, it's J-U-N-I-C-H-I.*
Sirpa: *And can I have your phone number?*
Junichi: *Yeah, it's five, five, five—one, two, three, four.*
Sirpa: *Last question: what's your e-mail address?*
Junichi: *My e-mail address is junichi-at-email-dot-com.*
Sirpa: *Do you prefer to be contacted by phone or by e-mail?*
Junichi: *E-mail. I'm hardly ever home to answer the phone.*

Model Conversation 2:

Sirpa: *Hi, Jenny. I'm making a class contact list. Can you spell your name for me?*
Jenny: *Sure, it's J-E-N-N-Y.*
Sirpa: *And can I have your phone number?*
Jenny: *Sorry, I'd rather not give that information out.*
Sirpa: *How about your e-mail address?*
Jenny: *No problem. My e-mail address is jenny-at-email-dot-com.*

INTERACTION LINK

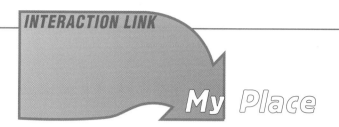

My Place

Describe your room to your partner and have him/her draw it as you describe it. Then draw your partner's room based on his or her description. Join with another pair and take turns describing the rooms in the pictures you drew.

MY ROOM

MY PARTNER'S ROOM

Model Conversation:

A: *What's your room like?*

B: *My room is nice and cozy. There is a small balcony. It has a nice view of the mountains.*

A: *That sounds really nice.*

Special Things

What special accessories do your classmates own?

Walk around your classroom. Ask at least 5 of your classmates or teacher what their accessories mean to them. Fill out this chart with what you find out.

It's a _____	It's a _____	It's a _____
I wear it/carry it because _____ _____ _____	I wear it/carry it because _____ _____ _____	I wear it/carry it because _____ _____ _____
It's a _____	It's a _____	It's a _____
I wear it/carry it because _____ _____ _____	I wear it/carry it because _____ _____ _____	I wear it/carry it because _____ _____ _____

Model Conversation:

A: *Excuse me, can you tell me about that pencil case? It's different. Is it an Egyptian mummy?*

B: *Oh, my best friend gave it to me. She got it at the Egyptian museum. I always carry it.*

After you have filled out the chart, tell a partner what you've learned.

A: *I think most people carry/wear something of sentimental value.*

B: *Really? I didn't find that.*

Find out how your classmates use their English.

- With a partner or in groups of three, write a questionnaire with three to five questions about how your classmates practice or study English outside class.

  Examples: *What do you do to practice outside of class?*
  How often do you watch movies in English (even with subtitles)?
  Do you have a favorite song in English? What are some of the words?

- Talk to as many classmates as you can. Ask them your survey questions.

- When you're finished, work with your partner or group again and make a graph of your findings.

- Present your findings in the class, or put your graphs on the wall where others can see them.

Model Conversation:

Paco: *Excuse me. Could I ask you some questions about learning English?*
Jung: *Sure.*
Paco: *What do you do to practice English outside of class?*
Jung: *Well, I talk to my friends in English, and listen to English music.*
Paco: *How often do you...?*

a sample graph

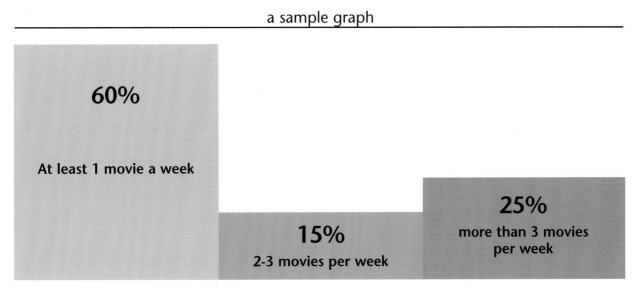

Movies: *How often do you watch movies in English?*

A Perfect Match

1. Choose one of the "personality profiles" below. (It doesn't have to be your real personality.)
2. Write down the characteristics.
3. Walk around the room and find your "ideal partner," according to your personality profile.
4. When you find your ideal partner, sit together and prepare to speak about the qualities you have in common.

Model Conversation 1:

A: Are you shy?
B: Yes. Do you like to listen to music?
A: Yeah, and I like listening to other people, too.
B: Hey, we're a good match!

Model Conversation 2:

A: Are you quiet?
B: No, I'm very talkative.
A: Maybe we're not a good match. Sorry.

Different types can go together:

"I'm outgoing and I like to talk. My partner likes to listen to people, so we think we make a good match."

Similar types can go together:

"I'm athletic, and my partner loves to exercise, so I think we make a good match."

You are a person who:	You are a person who:	You are a person who:	You are a person who:
1. Likes to play music 2. Is a little shy around people 3. Enjoys listening to people	1. Loves taking walks 2. Likes to talk about serious things 3. Is very honest	1. Is athletic 2. Likes to talk to people 3. Is outgoing	1. Loves to exercise 2. Is simple and honest 3. Likes quiet people
You are a person who:	**You are a person who:**	**You are a person who:**	**You are a person who:**
1. Seems quiet 2. Is intelligent 3. Is sensitive	1. Is not very outgoing 2. Likes to listen to music 3. Reads poetry	1. Loves cats 2. Is independent (likes to do things alone) 3. Likes being spontaneous	1. Loves dogs 2. Needs to be around other people 3. Has a great sense of humor
You are a person who:	**You are a person who:**	**You are a person who:**	**You are a person who:**
1. Is witty 2. Is outgoing 3. Plays music	1. Is sensitive 2. Has very complicated thoughts 3. Likes to listen to music	1. Loves life 2. Is talkative 3. Is spontaneous	1. Loves challenges 2. Takes risks 3. Likes computers

Something in Common

Walk around your class. Ask your classmates what they have in common with a family member. For example:

Appearance: *has the same eye color; has curly hair; is tall*
Personality: *is patient; has a lot of energy; gets along with everyone*
Hobbies: *likes chess; is good at skating; paints; reads*

Classmate's Name	Family Member	What They Have in Common
Angela	her sister	they listen to the same music
Randy	his dad	they like to work on cars

Model Conversation:

Randy: Hi, Angela. Who do you have something in common with?
Angela: I guess my sister.
Randy: Why is that?
Angela: She listens to the same music I do. She's always borrowing my CDs! How about you?
Randy: I think my dad and I have a lot in common.
Angela: Yeah? Like what?
Randy: We both like working on cars. He helped me rebuild the engine in my car last month.

Hide and Seek

How good are you at following and giving directions?

1. Choose a partner. Ask your partner to face the wall so he or she can't see what you're doing.

2. Place something of yours (a book, a pencil case…) on a desk or hide it around the classroom.

3. Tell your partner how to get from one side of the room to your object. When they get to the right place, switch roles. Hide three items each.

Use these words:

go down	until you get to	on your right/left
go to	turn right/left	on the other side of
go along	when you get to	across

Model Conversation:

Steve: *Go along the wall until you get to Tony's desk. Turn right and walk until you get to Seidy's desk.*

Alexandra: *OK, right at Tony's desk. Walk until Seidy's desk.*

Steve: *Turn left at Seidy's desk, then walk until you get to Peggy's desk.*

Alexandra: *Left at Seidy's desk, go to Peggy's desk. Oh, here's your pencil case across from Peggy's desk.*

Steve: *Great! Now it's your turn.*

Job Search

You've got a new job—now you have to guess what it is!

1. **Choose one of the jobs below. Write this job on a card and tape it on another student's back. Someone will stick a job card on your back. (Don't look at it!)**

2. **Walk around the room. Ask questions about your job and try to guess what it is.**

3. **When you think you know the job, ask:** *Am I a _____?*

Sample questions:

Do I work indoors or outdoors?   *What are the benefits (or advantages) of this job?*

Would you like to have this job?   *Do I make a high salary or a low salary?*

NURSE	NEWS ANNOUNCER	GARBAGE COLLECTOR	SCIENTIST
BALLET DANCER	CONSTRUCTION WORKER	MUSICIAN	COMPUTER PROGRAMMER
CASHIER	HOUSE PAINTER	SHIP PILOT	ARTIST
TELEPHONE OPERATOR	LAWYER	ACTOR/ACTRESS	ENGINEER
FLIGHT ATTENDANT	ELEPHANT TRAINER	WRITER	DOCTOR
ASTRONAUT	PRESIDENT	ENGLISH TEACHER	WINDOW-WASHER

When all your classmates have guessed their jobs, give a short summary of your job:

1. job name
2. where/how you work (inside/outside/with people)
3. salary (high/low/medium)
4. advantages, features

Model:

I'm an artist.

I work inside most of the time.

I make a low salary, but I like my job because I can be creative.

A Great Place to Visit

Create your own special place and write your own rules.
Form a group with your classmates. Decide what kind of place you want to create—for example, a school, a camp or a resort. Then write a brochure for it. Make five rules and list them on your brochure.

Example:

| THE BLAKE RANCH

A tradition of challenge

Knowmore, Arizona | At the Blake Ranch, you will learn how to ride and rope and talk like a cowboy.

It will be the most fun you've ever had! | AT THE BLAKE RANCH, YOU MUST FOLLOW THESE RULES:

1. Campers must wear cowboy boots at all times.

2. Campers have to remove cowboy hats when indoors.

3. Call the horses by their first names.

4. Do not leave saddles out in the rain.

5. Carry your lasso rope at all times. |

Your brochure:

| (name)

(slogan)

(place) | (description)

(sales pitch) |

(rules) |

When you've finished, put your brochure where your classmates can see it easily. Walk around and look at the brochures other groups have made. Choose the place you would like to visit. Which group got the most votes?

The Terrible Trip Game

1. Work in groups of three or four. Each player needs a small object for a game piece.

2. Place your game pieces on Start. Decide who will go first, then take turns moving around the board. (Close your eyes, point to a number on the number grid, then move forward the number of spaces your finger points to.)

3. Keep notes on a piece of paper. (What problems did you have? What did you do?)

4. Continue around until everyone has reached Finish.

5. Take turns describing your terrible trip. Your group will vote on the worst trip. The player who had the worst trip is the winner!

Model Conversation:

Janet: How was your trip, Arthur?

Arthur: Well, first I got delayed when there was a hurricane in Miami. Then I got lost going back to the hotel…

Janet: Wow, that's terrible!

Travel Notes

Miami hurricane - lost a turn

Start

Finish

Flight canceled. Lose a turn.

Flight delayed. Go back 1 space.

Upgrade to first class. Go ahead 2 spaces.

Forget your passport. Go back to Start.

Hotel. Take a rest.

You miss your flight. Lose 2 turns.

Weather gets bad. Airport closed, lose 2 turns.

Hotel. Take a rest.

You get lost. Lose a turn.

Luggage is missing. Go back 3 spaces.

Wallet stolen. Go back 2 spaces.

Win a free ticket to Paris. Go ahead 2 spaces.

Visa expires. Go to embassy to extend it. Lose a turn.

Rental car accident. Go back 2 spaces.

Hotel overbooked. Upgrade to suite. Take another turn.

Hotel. Take a rest.

Number Grid

3	1	3	4	2
1	4	2	3	1
2	3	4	2	3
4	1	2	4	1
3	2	1	2	4

Internet Business

Work in a small group to create your own Internet company.
1. **Look at the table and choose the kind of business you'd like to create.**
2. **Think of a name for your product or service.**
3. **Decide what makes your business special or useful.**
4. **Write a slogan for your product or service.** (Nike: *"Just do it."*)
5. **"Launch" your business by presenting your ideas to another group.**

banking	bakery	supermarket	fast food restaurant
flower shop	office supplies	clothes store	language school
coffee shop	taxi service	car company	travel agency

Our company's name:

Our product or service:

What makes us special:

Our slogan:

Model Presentation:

"Our company's name is WackyWidgets. We chose this name because it is easy to remember. Our product is a widget. It is useful for holding open doors. It is special because it comes in five see-through colors. Our slogan is: *Hold it open with a WackyWidget!* You can see our product on our website at www.wackywidgets.com.

Make a date with your classmates to do something fun!

1. Practice the conversation with a partner. Fill in the blanks with days, times and events.

Model Conversation:

A: *What are you doing on* _____(day)_____*? Are you free around* ____(time)____*?*

B: (choose an answer)

    a. *Sorry, I'm booked. Do you have any other days/times open?*

    b. *Things are kind of tight that day but maybe I can squeeze you in at* _(time)___*?*

    c. *Yeah, I'm free then. What do you have in mind?*

A: *Do you want to* _____ *with me?*

2. Now fill in 10 cards with events and times. You can write real or imaginary events.

Example: *Saturday 6:00 p.m. — Have dinner at McDonald's.*

Saturday -	**Saturday -**	**Saturday -**	**Saturday -**
Go to a party at	Have dinner at	Play tennis with	Have tea at
Saturday -	**Saturday -**	**Saturday -**	**Saturday -**
Go to movies to see	Play ___ at	Attend a meeting about	See a baseball game between ___ and
Sunday -	**Sunday -**	**Sunday -**	**Sunday -**
Go see ___ in concert.	Watch ___ on TV.	Have breakfast at	Go shopping at
Sunday -	**Sunday -**	**Sunday -**	**Sunday -**
Go play	Go to the park to	Volunteer at	

3. Walk around the class. Invite classmates to the events on your cards. When they accept, give them a card and write the event in your schedule below. Accept their invitations, too. Try to fill in your schedule with as many interesting activities as you can.

	SATURDAY	**SUNDAY**
Morning		
Afternoon		
Evening		

The Four Seasons Game

See how well you can use the weather words and idioms from this unit.

1. In a small group, cut out one complete set of the cards, mix them up, and put them face down on the table.

2. Use a coin for your marker. Put it on "Start." The player whose birthday is soonest goes first.

3. Take turns:
   a. Pick up the top card. Read the word or idiom on the card.
   b. Make a sentence using the word and write it on your paper.
   c. Move your marker to the next space for the season shown on the back of the card.

4. To win: Be the first player to get to "Finish." Have your teacher check your sentences to see if they are all right.

leaves	raining cats and dogs	crisp	cool
warm	have one's head in the clouds	breezy	rainy
flower blossoms	a fair-weather friend	sunny	breeze
save for a rainy day	chilly	showers	damp
hot	muggy	humid	wind
lightning	thunder	scorching	take a rain check
snow	snowed under	feeling under the weather	flurries
overcast	blizzard	freezing	ice

Fall	Fall	Fall	Fall
Fall	Fall	Fall	Fall
Spring	Spring	Spring	Spring
Spring	Spring	Spring	Spring
Summer	Summer	Summer	Summer
Summer	Summer	Summer	Summer
Winter	Winter	Winter	Winter
Winter	Winter	Winter	Winter

The Four Seasons Game continued from page 63

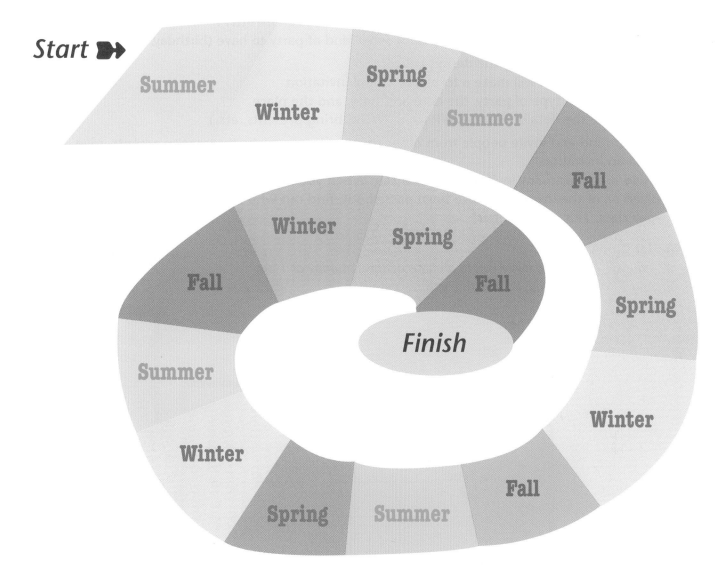

Start ➡

Summer · Winter · Spring · Summer · Fall · Winter · Fall · Spring · Winter · Spring · Fall · **Finish** · Summer · Fall · Winter · Spring · Summer

Words or Idioms I picked	Sentences
flurries	Yesterday there were snow flurries in my hometown.
1.	1.
2.	2.
3.	3.
4.	4.
5.	5.

Let's Party

Plan a party for this weekend (Friday, Saturday, or Sunday)!

1. With a partner or in a small group, decide what kind of party to have (birthday, cocktail, etc.).

2. Make 4 invitations using the design below.
   - decide if you will make a formal or casual invitation
   - fill in the type of party, the date and time, and the place
   - write the details (Place, RSVP to...., BYOB, bring presents, etc.)

3. Walk around and invite people from other groups to your party. If someone accepts, give them an invitation.

4. Try to accept as many invitations as you can. When you have a time conflict, refuse politely.

5. When all of the invitations have been passed out, find out who has the most invitations in your class. That's the winner!

Model Conversation:

Jeffrey: I'd like to invite you to a barbecue this Saturday at 1 pm.

Ana: Thank you, I'd love to come.

                   OR

    I'm sorry, I have other plans.

YOU'RE INVITED!

Type of Party: _____

Date and Time: _____

Place: _____

Details: _____

_____

_____

Space Station

With a partner or in a group, design your ideal space station.

• **Decide what kinds of living areas (rural, urban, suburban) you will have.**

• **Choose the conveniences you would like to have.**

• **Draw a picture or pictures of your space station.**

• **Pretend you are a reporter and interview other groups about their space stations.**

• **Describe your space station to others and answer their questions.**

Model Conversation:

Taira: *This is our space station. There is only a rural area because we like the outdoors. You can fish and swim in the rivers and lakes and go hiking in the mountains.*

Reporter 1: *Is there any public transportation?*

Taira: *No, only bicycles, horses, and wagons.*

Reporter 2: *Where do you buy food?*

Taira: *We grow our own food right here [points] in the fields.*

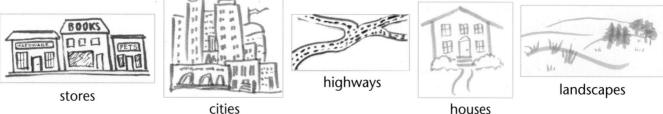

stores

cities

highways

houses

landscapes

Home Remedies

Many families have their own ways to treat common health problems. These are called *home remedies.*

Work in a group of three. Choose a box. Write your initials on the box. Tell your classmates what people in your family do to treat this problem. Continue until all the boxes are marked.

Then go to another group. Compare your answers. Which treatment do you think is the most effective? Which is the most unusual?

sore throat	hangover	hiccups	nerves (being nervous)
back pain	stomach pain	a cold	headache
muscle pain	sleeplessness (insomnia)	low energy (feeling run down)	tired eyes
toothache	coughing	earache	pimples

Let's Make a Deal

Act out a role-play with your partner.

Student A: You are a shopkeeper. You have no prices listed on your products. People who come to buy at your shop have to ask for the price. **Follow the model conversation to bargain. When the buyer gives you a price, ask for a little more until you arrive at the price that you think is fair. Your goal is to earn 20 Impact dollars.**

Student B: You want to get the lowest price for the item you choose. **Don't accept the first or second price the vendor gives you. Always offer a lower price, until you get a price you think is fair. Your goal is to get all of the items for 10 Impact dollars.**

Here are the items you want to buy:

| some cheese | basketball | umbrella | bananas | chair | a pair of gloves |

ONE Impact Dollar | **ONE** Impact Dollar | **ONE** Impact Dollar | **ONE** Impact Dollar | **ONE** Impact Dollar

ONE Impact Dollar | **ONE** Impact Dollar | **ONE** Impact Dollar | **ONE** Impact Dollar | **ONE** Impact Dollar

ONE Impact Dollar | **ONE** Impact Dollar | **ONE** Impact Dollar | **ONE** Impact Dollar | **ONE** Impact Dollar

ONE Impact Dollar | **ONE** Impact Dollar | **ONE** Impact Dollar | **ONE** Impact Dollar | **ONE** Impact Dollar

Model Conversation:

Seller: *Welcome! How can I help you today?*
Buyer: *How much is this cheese?*
Seller: *It's three Impact dollars a pack.*
Buyer: *You're kidding! Tell you what, I'll give you one Impact dollar for it.*
Seller: *A dollar? How about two fifty?*
Buyer: *One seventy-five.*
Seller: *I can't go any lower than two twenty-five.*
Buyer: *How about two dollars?*
Seller: *Okay, two Impact dollars.*

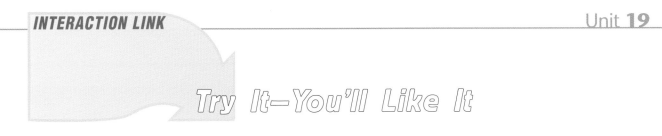

Cut out the cards below. Take two cards—one food card and one taste card.
Walk around the classroom. Your goals are to:
   a. **Give away your own food card to someone with a taste for that kind of food.**
   b. **Get a food card to match your taste card.**

Ask your classmates if they'd like to try the food you have. They will see if the taste matches the one on their card. If it does, give them the food card.

Continue. Keep going until you have five matches, or until your teacher asks you to stop.

Taste Cards:

I'm in the mood for something sweet.	I've got a taste for something juicy and hearty.	I feel like something spicy.	I'm in the mood for something chewy.	I feel like something bland.	I've got a taste for something light.
I've got a taste for something hot and spicy.	I'm in the mood for something salty.	I've got a craving for something a little sour.	I feel like something creamy.	I've got a craving for something really hot.	I've got a craving for chocolate.

Food Cards:

Steamed Crayfish with lemon These small lobster-like creatures are steamed and served with lemon slices. Their salty and sour flavor is very popular in Louisiana.	**Grilled Spicy Fish Paté in Banana Leaf** This is a salty paste made of fish, wrapped up in banana leaves. It's a typical portable lunch in Asia.
Moroccan Couscous Carrots, fennel, zucchini, and chickpeas in a spicy broth with jalapeños, caraway, and coriander make for a full-flavored couscous.	**Shrimp and Squid Noodles** Shrimp, chewy squid, strips of cooked egg and crisp bean sprouts spark this creamy, satisfying one-dish meal.
Ostrich Shish Kebabs Grilled pieces of ostrich meat are alternated with pieces of onion and salty bacon on long wooden skewers. Nice for a light snack.	**Sweet and Sour Onions** This dish is an excellent accompaniment for roasts and meat dishes and may be served cold as an antipasto. Vinegar in the sauce makes it tangy and slightly sour.
Banana Smoothie This cool, creamy, sweet and satisfying mixture is almost like a dessert you can drink!	**Chocolate Fudge Cake** Dark and rich chocolate flavor takes the cake with this one!
Vanilla Tofu Pudding This calming, bland dish will make you feel mellow after a long day.	**Wyoming Bison Burger** A thick, juicy cut of buffalo, which the Native Americans valued for providing food as well as clothing. For a hearty appetite.

News Debate

Think of some topics to debate. Work in teams of four.

Examples:

Guns - Guns are dangerous and should be banned.
Exercise - Students should be required to take exercise classes.
Language - English should be taught in elementary school in all countries.
Working Mothers - Mothers should wait until their children are of school age before they go to work outside the home.
Modern Families - People don't need to get married anymore to have children.

Students prepare to debate one of the topics in teams.

Structure for a debate:
A. Write three statements supporting your opinion.

1. _____

2. _____

3. _____

Model:

We believe that English should be taught in elementary school because experts say it is easier to learn languages at an early age.

B. Listen to what your opponent says. Write one question that challenges their opinion.
For example: *You said that . . . but don't you think that . . .?"*

1. _____

Model:

You said that it is too expensive to hire special English teachers for the elementary schools. The teachers working now could be replaced gradually by teachers who can teach English, or can be trained to teach English, as well as their other subjects.

C. Write a closing statement that summarizes your opinion and shows the weakness of the opponent's argument.

Model:

We believe that all countries should offer English in elementary schools because it is an international language and will help students to take their part as global citizens.

Real World Listening

Listen to the conversation. Fill in the missing parts.

before	handsome	met	Sam	want
broke	him	out	talk	who
December	introduce	party	telling	with
going	like	really	there	wish

Alice: Look, _____ he is.

Jean: _____ ?

Alice: Robert, the guy I've been _____ you about.

Jean: Oh, the guy you're _____ out with?

Alice: I _____ . The guy I _____ to go out with.

Jean: Oh, he's really _____ . Let's go _____ to him.

Alice: Oh, okay. I'll _____ you. I think you'll really _____ him ... Hi, Robert.

Robert: Oh, hi.

Alice: Have you _____ my friend, Jean?

Robert: Hey, Jean. I think we've _____ .

Jean: We have? _____ ?

Robert: Last _____ . At Sam's _____ .

Jean: Oh, _____ .

Robert: Oh? Aren't you going out with _____ anymore?

Jean: No, we _____ up a couple of months ago.

Robert: Oh... Oh, _____ ?

BONUS QUESTION

What do you think will happen next? Write more lines for the conversation.

74

Real World Listening

🔊 Listen to the conversation. Check (✔) the correct words.

Woman:	*Moshi-moshi. Gengo sentaa...*
Father:	Hello ...Hello ...Veronica ...Veronica...Veronica Smith... Is Veronica Smith (a) here (b) there, please?
Woman:	Ah, ah ... Veronica-*sensei* ... Veronica-*sensei*? Wait a moment, please ...
Father:	Wait a moment? What's (a) happening (b) going on ?
Veronica:	Hello.
Father:	Hello, Veronica? (a) Is that you (b) Are you there ?
Veronica:	Yes, Dad. (a) I'm here (b) It's me.
Father:	Where is this place? Somebody was speaking Japanese to me. I mean, did I call the (a) right (b) wrong number?
Veronica:	Dad, you called the (a) home (b) school number. And you're lucky I'm here now. Dad, I (a) asked (b) told you. Don't call the school number. (a) Remember (b) Do you remember ?
Father:	Yes, but you (a) refused to give me (b) didn't give me your home phone number. Why didn't you (a) call (b) contact me?
Veronica:	I just got here a (a) week (b) few days ago... Okay, let me (a) tell (b) give it to you. Are you ready?
Father:	Ready. Ready. Okay.
Veronica:	Okay. It's (a) 798-55-4123 (b) 789-55-4213.
Father:	(a) 798-55-4123 (b) 789-55-4213.
Veronica:	Oh, oh, wait. Dial the (a) city (b) country code. And that's 81 ... and then ... and then the number.
Father:	Why is the number (a) wrong (b) so long ?
Veronica:	Because it is, Dad.
Father:	Do you have a (a) job (b) place yet?
Veronica:	Yeah. Let me give you (a) the name (b) the address. Are you ready?
Father:	Uh ... yeah. Okay. (a) What (b) What is it?
Veronica:	It's one dash one dash one fifty-five ... Uegahara B356.
Father:	Wait. Wait. One...one what? (a) Is it (b) Why is it so long?
Veronica:	Dad, I've got to go. I'll send it to you (a) by mail (b) by e-mail. Bye.
Father:	But ...what's your (a) home address (b) e-mail address?

BONUS QUESTION

Imagine you are Veronica. Write a journal entry about your relationship with your father.

Real World Listening

🔘 **Listen to the conversation. Put the lines in order.**

Diane: _____ Look at this furniture. It's so modern. I feel so elegant here.

John: _____ What's wrong with our place?

Diane: _____ Isn't this place fantastic?

John: _____ You do? I feel like I'm in a museum. It's so phony, so uncomfortable. Are you supposed to sit in these chairs?

John: _____ Oh, gosh. It makes me seasick. Our place is so much more down-to-earth.

Diane: _____ Oh, John, don't you wish we could live in a place like this?

John: _____ It must be cold in the winter. Our place is so cozy and warm.

Diane: _____ It's so big. So spacious. So much room. I feel so. . . free here.

Diane: _____ Oh, John! And the view! Look at the view of the ocean from this window! I feel so relaxed.

John: _____ Well, I don't know. I mean, it's okay.

BONUS QUESTION

When John and Diane return home later in the evening, what will they talk about? Write a dialogue.

Real World Listening

🔘 **Listen to the conversation. Fill in the missing parts.**

an old woman in our village	I put it on	since you were little
because I was a girl	I remembered the necklace	so that I could get better
But you know what?	I started to get sick again	take it off
didn't want to treat me	I took it off	took me to a doctor
had this silver necklace made	I was fine	took me to this witch doctor
I don't believe that	I was a kid	went to a jeweler
I needed silver	sick all the time	

Jean: I'm ready. Are you? Why don't you take that necklace off before you go in the pool?

Chandra: Oh, this? No, I never _____. I wear it all the time. I've had it since _____.

Jean: Really? You've worn it _____? Why?

Chandra: Well, when I was a baby, I lived in India. And I was _____, so my parents _____. And, well, the doctor at first _____...

Jean: What? Why?

Chandra: Well, _____.

Jean: Huh? Because you were a girl?

Chandra: Yeah, well, that's the way it was. Anyway, so my parents _____, and I...

Jean: A witch doctor?

Chandra: Yeah, well, I guess you could call her a ... I don't know, a spiritual healer. She was _____. And she took a look at me and she said _____.

Jean: Silver?

Chandra: Yeah. She said I needed silver _____. And then my grandmother _____ and she _____ for me. They put it on me, and I got better.

Jean: _____.

Chandra: Well, I didn't either for a while. _____ When I was 20, _____ and I put it into a drawer for a little while. And then _____. And I didn't get better. I was just sick all the time. And then _____, and _____. And after that, _____.

Jean: Wow.

BONUS QUESTION

What do you think about this story? Write your opinion.

Real World Listening

Listen to the conversation. Choose the correct words.

Cindy: What the heck is that?

Dave: It's a Thai (a) magazine (b) newspaper.

Cindy: Thai? You can (a) speak (b) read Thai?

Dave: Well, (a) a little (b) not so much.

Cindy: How?

Dave: I went to (a) Bangkok (b) Thailand last summer and I lived with (a) a Thai friend and his family (b) a friend of a Thai family. I had such a (a) good time (b) great experience I want to go back.

Cindy: Why? (a) What (b) How was your experience like?

Dave: Well, I started to learn some Thai... and (a) practiced (b) started talking with people and (a) ordering in (b) going to restaurants and everybody was (a) so nice (b) very friendly... you know, Thailand is called (a) the Land of the Smiles (b) the Palace of the Styles ... they even smiled when I (a) tried to speak (b) made a mistake speaking the language. The people were (a) great (b) beautiful. Everything was beautiful. It (a) changed me (b) changed my life.

Cindy: But I've always heard that Thai was (a) difficult (b) impossible to learn.

Dave: Maybe for some people, but (a) it wasn't (b) not for me. I mean it is (a) a little (b) totally different from English. The (a) writing system (b) way of writing is different, they use different (a) pronunciation (b) tones, everything's different, but I really (a) hope to understand it (b) want to learn it. I want to understand more when I (a) go back (b) study it.

Cindy: I wish I felt that way about (a) studying English (b) learning French. Maybe I should (a) give up (b) study another language.

Dave: No, Cindy, it's not the language. You've just got to (a) try harder (b) get into it.

BONUS QUESTION

What do you think of Dave's ideas about learning a foreign language?

Real World Listening

🔘 **Listen to the conversation. Fill in the missing parts.**

but he has a nice smile	How can you tell	Not really	the neatest guy
cry at movies	he just cried	over the weekend	this really sad part
Does he work out a lot	like about him	really romantic movie	try to hide it
Handsome	more than that	sensitive	you like that
He's kind of cute	Not especially	sweet	what's he like

Sheri: Hey, I went out with _____ _____ !

Jeremy: Yeah, _____ ? Tall? _____ ?

Sheri: _____ .

Jeremy: Dress nice? Drive a nice car?

Sheri: _____ .

Jeremy: Then he must be buff. _____ ?

Sheri: No, _____ . Dimples. I like dimples.
_____ .

Jeremy: And that's what you _____ ?

Sheri: No, it's _____ . He's _____ .

Jeremy: Sensitive? _____ ?

Sheri: Well, we went to this _____ , and there was
_____ , and he ... cried.

Jeremy: He cried?

Sheri: Yeah, _____ and he didn't _____
or anything. It was so _____

Jeremy: Oh, _____ huh? Well, I _____ ,
too!

BONUS QUESTION
Make up a similar conversation. Write a conversation between two friends about a date.

Real World Listening

Listen to the conversation. Choose the correct words.

Nate: Are these your (a) parents (b) folks ?

Jane: Yeah, that's my (a) whole family (b) wonderful family.

Nate: Hmm. You look a lot like your (a) dad (b) mom ... especially your eyes. Very deep, (a) lovely (b) beautiful eyes.

Jane: Oh, thank you...

Nate: And the same figure ... same (a) size (b) shape.

Jane: Uh, hey, I don't want to hear that. I may (a) act like (b) look like my mom, but I really (a) think like (b) take after my dad.

Nate: Really, (a) how (b) in what way ?

Jane: We're both very (a) attractive (b) adventurous. My dad was, like, (a) into (b) interested in motorcycles when he was younger ... he was in one of those, you know, motorcycle (a) clubs (b) groups.

Nate: You mean, like a motorcycle gang?

Jane: Yeah, but that was (a) before he was married (b) before he had children. I've been (a) driving (b) riding a motorcycle myself since I was 17.

Nate: You? (a) No (b) No way!

Jane: Yeah, I've always done (a) things (b) stuff like that.

Nate: Really, like what else?

Jane: Well, (a) skating (b) surfing, (a) snowboarding (b) skiing ... My dad and I even went (a) bike-riding (b) skydiving once. We didn't tell (a) my mom (b) my dad, though. She would have (a) liked (b) killed us!

BONUS QUESTION
In what ways do you take after your mom? Your dad? Someone else? Explain.

Real World Listening

🔘 **Listen to Paula's story. Fill in the missing parts.**

alone for a change	got really scared	suddenly
comes up to me	group tour	the whole time I traveled
decide which one to go to	haven't been so afraid	there we were
decided to follow him	I'd just better leave	try to find a restaurant
ended up being	out of the hotel	was in
ever since then	sort of adventurous	what was going on
go out on our own	stay with the group	

Paula: I _____ Istanbul once, part of this
_____, and the tour guide told us to always
_____, not to _____. But one night (coughs)
I was feeling _____, and I thought I'd _____
and eat dinner _____. So I walked _____ by
myself. I was looking around at all the restaurants and I couldn't _____.
And this little Turkish man _____ and he says, "My nephew has a good
restaurant. Come with me." So I _____. And we went down these
little streets ... and back ... and it was getting dark ... back alleys, and I didn't know
_____. People were starting to stare at me. And I
_____. And I thought, " _____ " So I was
going to run. And then _____ we rounded the corner and
_____ at the restaurant. And it _____ the best
Turkish food I had _____. And _____,
I _____ to take chances.

BONUS QUESTION
Have you ever had an unusual experience while traveling? Write about it.

Real World Listening

Listen to the interview. Choose the correct words.

Interviewer:	So, Ms. Spencer, why (a) did you apply (b) have you applied for this job at CNN?
Amy:	Well, I've always (a) hoped (b) wanted to be a journalist and I (a) like (b) enjoy traveling. And you can (a) meet (b) interview lots of important people.
Interviewer:	Tell me about your (a) background (b) experience in journalism.
Amy:	Um ... well, I (a) make (b) create a newsletter for my family. And I worked on my high school (a) newspaper (b) yearbook. And I read a lot of newspapers and (a) news magazines (b) gossip magazines ...
Interviewer:	Do you think you're (a) qualified (b) prepared for the prestige of this job?
Amy:	Absolutely. I've taken (a) journalism (b) acting lessons. And I look (a) good (b) great on camera. And I (a) read (b) travel a lot so I think I'd be good as a (a) news broadcaster (b) foreign correspondent.
Interviewer:	What about (a) cooperation (b) teamwork? Have you ever (a) participated (b) worked as part of a team?
Amy:	Of course. I was really great at (a) sports (b) teamwork in high school and...
Interviewer:	You don't seem to have much experience as a (a) writer (b) journalist.
Amy:	Well, that's not exactly true. I write a lot of (a) news stories (b) e-mail to my friends.
Interviewer:	And you haven't taken any (a) communications (b) journalism courses, have you?
Amy:	Well, I took a class in modern film, and one in communications, or something like that.
Interviewer:	Well, thanks, Ms. Spencer. We'll (a) call you (b) be in touch.

BONUS QUESTION
Rewrite the dialogue. Change the information that Amy gives to help her get the job.

Real World Listening

🔊 **Listen to the conversation. Put the lines in order.**

Cathy:	_____ Isolated? What do you mean?
Kevin:	_____ It says here there's no TV and you can't use any electrical appliances.
Cathy:	_____ Uh-huh...
Kevin:	_____ Hey, Cathy, I found a good place for a vacation this summer.
Cathy:	_____ So you're telling me there's no TV, no computers, and I have to wake up every morning to go hiking. Why on earth would anybody want to go there?
Kevin:	_____ I think it would be relaxing. I'd like to get away from the phone for a week. And I think it'd be good for you.
Cathy:	_____ Ahh. Sounds like work.
Kevin:	_____ It's called Camp Star.
Cathy:	_____ Hmm. Looks pretty. But what can you do there?
Kevin:	_____ It's kind of isolated.
Cathy:	_____ No TV? And no electrical ... Wait a minute. What about my notebook computer?
Kevin:	_____ It's off the coast, and you have to take a boat to get there. This week's program is that you hike and hear lectures and talk about current issues.
Cathy:	_____ What is it?
Kevin:	_____ No, it's an old hotel. They have a couple of rules, though.
Cathy:	_____ Where do you stay? Tents?
Kevin:	_____ No, no computers, and there's only one telephone on the whole island.
Cathy:	_____ What? So I won't be able to check my e-mail either?
Kevin:	_____ You'll get by. It'll be fun! Look, you can read, and talk, and think. And every morning you go for a long hike.

BONUS QUESTION

Imagine that Cathy and Kevin have arrived at Camp Star. They are having a conversation after their first day at the island. Write the dialogue.

Real World Listening

Listen to the conversation. Fill in the missing parts.

broke into my house	going to Costa Rica	stay overnight	was really nice
didn't have my passport	go into the airline office	the next day	we got married
get to	had a terrible time getting there	this really wonderful woman	we sort of hit it off
got to the airport	had to stop in Mexico City	your luggage isn't there	we had engine trouble
got my passport	missed that flight	was stuck there	wouldn't even let us

Angela: I'm thinking about _____ .

Trevor: Great. I went to Costa Rica once — but I _____

Angela: Oh, yeah? Well, what happened?

Trevor: Well, when I _____ , I realized I _____ .

Angela: Oh, no.

Trevor: So I called a friend, and he _____ , _____
            and brought it to me. But I _____ so I had to
            _____ in San Francisco.

Angela: Oh, that's too bad.

Trevor: Yeah. So I got the flight _____ , and of course on the way
            _____ , so we _____ . And I
            _____ for another, like, 22 hours while they got the part.

Angela: Oh, my gosh!

Trevor: And I mean stuck. They _____ out of the airport.

Angela: You're kidding!

Trevor: I'm telling you. So finally, we, like, after all this time, I _____
            Costa Rica two days late and —

Angela: And don't tell me: _____ .

Trevor: You guessed it. I _____ to complain and there was
            _____ working at the counter.

Angela: Oh, yeah?

Trevor: And she _____ and helped me out ...

Angela: Mm-hmm ...

Trevor: And _____ ...

Angela: Yeah? And then what?

Trevor: About two months later _____ !

BONUS QUESTION
Retell Trevor's story. Add 5 new details.

Real World Listening

Listen to the conversation. Fill in the missing parts.

a lot of stuff in here	I type on the keyboard	to want to watch them all day
are you selling a lot of disks	of doing my work	you just watch these
be more disciplined	put on the web page	what is all this stuff
for the different types of things	scan in graphics	what are these things
got your own business	shipping out orders	what are all these boxes for
have to check out the DVDs	so I can talk on the phone	what's this big thing
I sell them	things are looking better all the time	

Leon: Come in! Andy! Hi!

Andy: Hey, are you ready to go? Pat and Chris are in the car. Let's go — Hey, _____ ?

Leon: This is my home office.

Andy: Whoa! You've got _____ .

Leon: Yeah, well, I need it all _____ I do for my business.

Andy: You've _____ ?

Leon: Yep. DivineDVDs.com. I got 50,000 hits on my website so far this week.

Andy: Cool. And you need all this stuff?

Leon: Oh, yeah, absolutely! This is my headset _____ to my customers while _____ .

Andy: Uh-huh. Uh-huh. And _____ next to your computer?

Leon: That's my scanner. I _____ and pictures to _____ .

Andy: I see. Oh, cool ... And _____ ?

Leon: Those are my DVD players. I've got four of them. I _____ before _____ , you know.

Andy: Uh-huh. So _____ , uh, DVDs all day?

Leon: Well, yeah. I have to _____ , though. You know, it's easy _____ instead _____ .

Andy: Yeah. And _____ ?

Leon: Those cardboard boxes? They're for _____ .

Andy: Sounds busy. So _____ ?

Leon: Um, no, not yet. But _____ .

BONUS QUESTION
What is a good idea for a home business? Describe how the business would be successful.

Real World Listening

Listen to the conversation. Correct the mistakes.

Manager: Okay, time to wake up women! Your fans are waiting for you!

Woman 1:   Huh? What day is it?

Manager: It's Tuesday. We're in Middleburg, Ohio, tonight, at the Summer Fest in the town stadium.

Woman 2:   Yeah. I hope it doesn't snow.

Manager: Then tomorrow it's up to New York to play for Sarah's induction into the Hall of Fame, followed by an autograph-signing session.

Woman 1:   I wish it was us being inducted. The first all-girl rock band in the Music Hall of Fame ... What's on for tomorrow?

Manager: Friday we have to be in the hotel in Akron. We're doing a live online chat on NBC TV. Come on, guys. You'll love it. It's at 12:00, and then we're in the Starlight Dome that evening.

Woman 1:   Where are we playing Saturday?

Manager: Cleveland, the Waterfront Fair. We'll be there Sunday night, too.

Woman 2:   This schedule is crazy. When do we get some time off?

Manager: Hah! We're booked through Sunday, but we have an easy schedule on Monday. We just have to fly out to record the new CD in Los Angeles, but at least you can sleep on the plane. Hmm?

BONUS QUESTION
Make a weekly schedule for the rock band that includes all of their events.

Real World Listening

Listen to the conversation. Choose the correct words.

Alex:	Grandma, what are these pictures?
Grandma:	These are pictures of Alaska.
Alex:	That's where you (a) grew up (b) were raised, right?
Grandma:	That's right, dear. I lived there until I was (a) 16 (b) 19 years old.
Alex:	Is that you in this picture?
Grandma:	Yes, that's me and my (a) cousin (b) sister, Ruth, and our dog, Kusko. That was out behind our house.
Alex:	Wow. It looks cold!
Grandma:	Yes, that was in the (a) fall (b) winter ... and it was cold ... it snowed (a) a lot (b) all the time! And boy, Kusko (a) was crazy about (b) just loved the snow. Ruth and I and Kusko used to play in the snow for hours.
Alex:	Did you make snowmen?
Grandma:	Oh, we made some (a) wonderful (b) great snowmen.
Alex:	Is that you in this picture, too?
Grandma:	Yes, that's me and Ruth again. I guess we were both in (a) high school (b) college then.
Alex:	Where are you?
Grandma:	We were (a) hiking (b) walking near Seward. We hiked a lot in those days.
Alex:	But where's the snow?
Grandma:	Well, it doesn't snow (a) all the time (b) at all in Alaska, you know. That was in the springtime. Spring was a great time for hiking. It was a little (a) slippery (b) muddy, though.

Alex:	Oh ...
Grandma:	Look, here's a picture of Ruth now, outside her house.
Alex:	That's Aunt Ruth's house, in Alaska? I thought everybody lived (a) in houses (b) in igloos!
Grandma:	Oh, no. Most people live in (a) wooden (b) regular houses! Aren't those flowers lovely?
Alex:	You mean, flowers grow there, too?
Grandma:	Of course. In the (a) spring (b) summer, everything just (a) grows (b) blooms. It's sunny and the weather is warm ...
Alex:	Warm? You mean, it was warm enough to go swimming?
Grandma:	Oh, we all went swimming in (a) the summer (b) July and August. The water was cold, but swimming was so much fun ...
Alex:	Was summer your favorite season?
Grandma:	You know, I love all the seasons, but I think my favorite season was (a) summer (b) autumn. The (a) trees (b) leaves in the mountains turning to gold. I always loved that (a) picture (b) sign of the changing seasons. Look, here's a picture of the (a) hills (b) mountains near our house in the fall.
Alex:	Wow, Grandma, I'd like to go to Alaska sometime.
Grandma:	Well, Alex, I've got an idea. Let's go to Alaska together sometime.
Alex:	Yeah, Grandma, that'd be great.

BONUS QUESTION

What is your favorite season? Why?

Real World Listening

🔘 **Listen to Katherine's story. Fill in the missing parts.**

a good impression	get out of	next weekend
a small company	he's invited me	really boring
avoid him	I didn't mind	seem rude
comes up to me	I've got tickets	this is all right
corners me	kind of weird	to get to know
couldn't say no	made it through	wanted to leave
Do you want to go	my boss	

I just started working at _____, and I want to make

_____. One day _____ comes up to me and

says "_____ to the Lakers basketball game on Sunday.

_____?" I don't know anything about basketball, but he said he want-

ed me _____ the other people in the office, and I didn't want to

_____, so I went, "Sure, I'll go." It was okay, because there were other

people from the office at the game. So _____. But the next time I see

him, he _____ and says, "Want to go to the opera

_____? I have an extra ticket." I was like, Okay, that's

_____, but I thought, well, maybe _____.

I've never been to an opera.   And so we went to the opera, but it was all in Italian, and it got

to be _____. But I sat through the whole show.

I _____ but he's my boss, so I _____. I didn't

feel like I could leave. So after that I tried to _____ in the office and I

almost _____ the week when he _____ yester-

day in the break room. And now _____ to go to the ballet. I hate the

ballet! How do I _____ this situation?

BONUS QUESTION

Have you ever been in an awkward situation like this? What did you do? Why?

Real World Listening

Listen to the interview. Correct the mistakes.

Sean: This is Sean McCain, live with Julie Morris, from Gemini One, the American space station. Julie, can you hear me?

Julie: Yes, I can hear you.

Sean: Julie, can you tell us: what is it like living on the Gemini One?

Julie: The Gemini One is awful. It's very different from living on Earth, really. We don't have jobs, friends, entertainment, natural beauty. And we have none of the modern conveniences that you have on Earth.

Sean: What modern conveniences?

Julie: Well, we have movie theaters, game centers, dance clubs, shops, restaurants...

Sean: How about food? How do you buy your food?

Julie: I go shopping, just like everyone here. You can get most types of food here.

Sean: Is food cheap?

Julie: Some of it is. The stuff that's exported to earth is very expensive. Like a loaf of bread from Earth can cost $1000. But most food is really cheap.

Sean: Do you miss getting away to the beach or the mountains? Don't you miss nature?

Julie: Well, we have lots of nature up here. I can go hiking and mountain biking, riding in the hills, take a swim in a beautiful ocean. It's really beautiful up here.

Sean: How do people travel up there?

Julie: Oh, just like we do down there. We have gasoline-powered cars and trains... but not airplanes.

Sean: What do you like most about living in the space station?

Julie: Well, the air is dirty. There's no pollution, and it's easy to get around. It's really a perfect world.

Sean: And what do you like least?

Julie: Well, it's kind of difficult to fly home to Earth to see my parents for the holidays.

BONUS QUESTION
Imagine you live on a space station. Write a journal entry. Describe a typical day in your life.

Real World Listening

Listen to the exercise. Choose the correct words.

OK, sit (a) down (b) back in your chair.

And let your hands rest (a) lightly (b) loosely in your lap.

Close your eyes. Now (a) lift (b) raise your shoulders up and then let them fall.

(a) Inhale   (b) Breathe in, filling your lungs with air.

Now (a) breathe out (b) let your breath out very slowly.

(a) Pretend (b) Imagine you are (a) in a forest (b) on a beach.

See the sand, the trees, and the water. Feel the soft (a) earth (b) sand below

you. Let your (a) body (b) feet sink into the sand.

Look at the gentle (a) waves (b) surface in the water.

The waves are (a) coming in   (b) going in ... and going out.

You're breathing (a) slowly (b) quickly and calmly, like the waves.

Feel the warm (a) air (b) sun on your (a) body (b) skin.

Oh, you feel good. You're (a) relaxed (b) asleep.

You're (a) healthy (b) well and happy.

Now, see yourself slowly (a) entering (b) leaving the beach.

Your body is warm and (a) rested (b) relaxed.

You come back to your (a) daily life (b) daily routine with new (a) life (b) energy and joy.

And now, slowly open your eyes.

BONUS QUESTION

Describe a scene that makes you feel relaxed and happy.

Real World Listening

🔊 **Listen to the conversation. Fill in the missing parts.**

a vegetable market	different languages	smells and bright colors
a little	fruit, eggs, spices, candy	some of it
all sorts of things here	from all over the place	what they have in their booths
at the market over there	Homemade sausage	what they're saying
bargaining is a must	Is it expensive	What do they sell here
Clothing, toiletries, hardware, electronics	Let's get some	what you want
	Shopping here is so exciting	Why are they all yelling

Amy: Wow this place is great! There are so many different _____ ...
What's that?

Peggy: _____. It's great for sandwiches. _____
for lunch.

Amy: I thought this was _____.

Peggy: Yeah, it is, but you can get _____ : _____ ...

Amy: Can I get batteries here?

Peggy: No, but we can get that _____. Let's go.

Amy: _____ ?

Peggy: They're telling everyone _____.

Amy: Can you understand _____ ?

Peggy: Well, _____. There are people _____ —
Senegal, Nigeria, Cape Verde ... So they're speaking _____.

Amy: _____ ?

Peggy: _____, you name it.

Amy: _____ ?

Peggy: No, it's pretty reasonable.

Amy: Okay. I want to get batteries for my Walkman and a new pair of pants.

Peggy: Okay, just point to _____. Oh, one more thing,
_____. When they tell you a price, offer half of what they ask.

Amy: Will they come down that far?

Peggy: No, but they'll come down _____.

Amy: Wow! _____ !

BONUS QUESTION
What is the most unusual place you know to go shopping. Describe it.

Real World Listening

Listen to the conversation. Put the lines in order.

Sandy: _____ What do you mean?

Jim: _____ Aren't you afraid of getting sick?

Sandy: _____ An ostrich burger! It tastes a lot like chicken.

Jim: _____ But that's raw! Is it still alive?

Sandy: _____ I guess I got used to it. You should try it. It's good for you.

Sandy: _____ Oh, I got the dancing shrimp on the side.

Jim: _____ I doubt it. Want some of my fries?

Sandy: _____ Mmm ... It's good. What is it?

Jim: _____ I did have octopus once — it didn't have that much taste. And it was too rubbery.

Jim: _____ Here, take a bite of this.

Sandy: _____ You don't know what you're missing. If you tried the dancing shrimp, I'm sure
you'd change your mind.

Jim: _____ Yeah, chewy! Like an eraser. Oh no, what's that?

Sandy: _____ Yeah. I like the mild salty flavor.

Jim: _____ With — what is that — octopus and squid? You call that usual? How can you eat
that stuff?

Sandy: _____ Ooh, too salty for me. And you think raw seafood is dangerous!

Jim: _____ I've heard that raw seafood is dangerous.

Sandy: _____ My usual, pizza. Want a bite?

Jim: _____ It's an ostrich burger.

Sandy: _____ It's just really chewy. It doesn't have that much flavor, really.

Jim: _____ Yeah, kind of strange to be eating ostrich, but it's excellent. What have you got?

BONUS QUESTION
What are some unusual foods in your culture? What are they like?

Real World Listening

Listen to the discussion again. Fill in the missing parts. (Use the correct form of the verbs.)

be	excel	hurt	let down	pressure	sit
be sensitive	feel	learn	make decisions	push	start
discuss	go	let	need	put	think
do	have fun	let	play	read	try
encourage	hear	let	pressure	read	want

Teacher: So, what do you _____ about parents _____ too much

pressure on their kids? Should they _____ them?

_____ some of your opinions. Anybody? Christina?

Student 1: I see lots of parents _____ to teach their kids _____ before

they _____ to school. They should just _____ their kids

_____ and _____ before they _____ school. If

the kids don't start _____ or whatever early, they'll

_____ bad, like they _____ their parents. They're only

_____ their children by _____ them _____ before they

_____ ready.

Teacher: Good idea. Eric, how about you?

Student 2: You know, parents _____ what's best for their children. I mean, kids

_____ their parents _____ for them at such a young age.

Without a little push from their parents, kids just _____ in front of

their TV sets or their computer games all day. So I think parents should

_____ their kids a little, but _____ to their needs, too. I

mean, they should _____ them play some of the time!

Teacher: Great idea. How about you, Julia?

Student 3: Maybe if they just _____ the kids _____ some of what

they want and then _____ them to get better at it ... and

_____ at the things they like.

Teacher: All great ideas. Now let's get into our groups and _____ this.

BONUS QUESTION

What is a current issue in the news? Write three different opinions about it.

Notes

Notes

Welcome to the *Impact* Series

■ **Coursebooks**

■ **Conversation courses**

■ **Skills courses**

Visit our website for more ideas and teacher discussion.

www.impactseries.com